PASS PMP IN 21 DAYS III - ITTO + KEYWORDS

Step III: SMART Memorize

KAVITA SHARMA

ACP, AgileBA, PMP, RMP, PRINCE2

BASED ON THE NEW PMP CONTENT 2022
VERSION: 7, RELEASED ON: 15 June 2022

Copyright © 2022 by Kavita Sharma

All rights reserved. No part of this book may be used or reproduced by any means.

Graphics, Electronic or Mechanical, including photocopying, recording, taping, or any information storage retrieval system without the author's written permission except in the case of brief quotations embodied in critical articles and reviews.

Because of the dynamic nature of the Internet, any web address or links contained in the book may have changed since publication and may no longer be valid.

A SINCERE GRATITUDE

I want to thank all my students for making this book possible and continue updating it. This is the 7th version of the book in your hands.

Your feedback emails/WhatsApp keep me motivated.

Thanks to all of you.

कर्मण्येवाधिकारस्ते मा फलेषु कदाचन ।

मा कर्मफलहेतुर्भुर्मा ते संगोऽस्त्वकर्मणि ॥

It is the work that you control and not the outcome.

Table of Contents

1. Process Chart and Formulas 5
   - Process Chart 6
   - PMP Formulas 7
   - EVM Formulas 8

2. Process ITTOS - Tabular format 9
   - Integration Management 10
   - Scope Management 11
   - Schedule Management 12
   - Cost Management 13
   - Quality Management 14
   - Resource Management 15
   - Communications Management 16
   - Risk Management 16
   - Procurement Management 18
   - Stakeholder Management 19

3. Process ITTO - Mindmaps 20
   - Integration Management 21
   - Scope Management 29
   - Schedule Management 36
   - Cost Management 43
   - Quality Management 48
   - Resource Management 52
   - Communications Management 59
   - Risk Management 63
   - Procurement Management 71
   - Stakeholder Management 75

4. Agile Overview and Key Terms 80
   - Agile Overview 81

5. Keywords - Tools and Techniques 85

6. About Kavita Sharma 89

1. PROCESS CHART AND FORMULAS

PROCESS CHART

	INITIATING	PLANNING	EXECUTING	MONITORING & CONTROLLING	CLOSING
INTEGRATION	Develop Project Charter	Develop Project Management Plan	Direct & Manage Project Work Manage Project Knowledge	Monitor & Control Project Work Perform Integrated Change Control	Close Project or Phase
SCOPE		Plan Scope Management Collect Requirements Define Scope Create WBS		Validate Scope Control Scope	
SCHEDULE		Plan Schedule Management Define Activities Sequence Activities Estimate Activity durations Develop Schedule		Control Schedule	
COST		Plan Cost Management Estimate Costs Determine Budget		Control Costs	
QUALITY		Plan Quality Management	Manage Quality	Control Quality	
RESOURCES		Plan Resource Management Estimate Activity Resources	Acquire Resources Develop Team Manage Team	Control Resources	
COMMUNICATIONS		Plan Communications Management	Manage Communications	Monitor Communications	
RISK		Plan Risk Management Identify Risks Perform Qualitative Risk Analysis Perform Quantitative Risk Analysis Plan Risk Responses	Implement Risk Responses	Monitor Risks	
PROCUREMENT		Plan Procurement Management	Conduct Procurements	Control Procurements	
STAKEHOLDER	Identify Stakeholders	Plan Stakeholder Management	Manage Stakeholder Engagement	Monitor Stakeholder Engagement	

1. Process Chart and Formulas

PMP FORMULAS

Group	Term/ Formula	What is it	Abbreviations
Portfolio Management	Net Present Value(NPV) The current value of future money.	Formula: $PV = FV/(1 + r)^t$ Select Highest	r = Interest rate PV = Present Value FV = Future Value t = Time period
	Opportunity Cost	The value of the project not selected	The second best project.
Schedule	Critical Path	The critical path is the sequence of activities representing the longest path through a project, determining the shortest possible project duration.	CPM
	Total Float	The amount of time that an activity can be delayed from its early start day without delaying the project finish date. Total Float = Late Start (Node) – Early Start (Node)	FLOAT
Three-Point Estimates	PERT / BETA Distribution	Mean = (P + 4M + O)/ 6	P- Pessimistic
	Average/ Triangular Distribution	Mean = (P + M + O)/3	O - Optimistic M - Most Likely
Quality	Standard Deviation	(Pessimistic – Optimistic) / 6	
	Variance	[(Pessimistic – Optimistic) / 6]2 Standard Deviation * Standard Deviation	Square of Standard Deviation
	Six Sigma Values	1 Sigma = 68.26% 2 Sigma = 95.46% 3 Sigma = 99.73% 6 Sigma = 99.99%	
	Control Limit	Control Limits = 3 sigma from mean	
Communications	Communication Channels	[N (N - 1)] / 2	N - No of stakeholders
Risk	Expected Monetary Value	(EMV) = Impact * Probability	
Estimates Range	Definitive Estimate	+10% to -5%	
	ROM or Rough Order of Magnitude Estimates	+175% to -75%	

EVM FORMULAS

TERM	Name	Formula	Gives Answers of:	Interpretation/Remarks
BAC	Budget at Completion	No formula	Approved Budget	
PV	Planned Value	BAC* Planned % Complete	What your schedule says you should have earned	
EV	Earned Value	BAC * Actual% Complete	How much of the project's value you've really earned	
AC	Actual Cost	No Formula	Actual spending on the projects	
SPI	Schedule Performance Index	SPI = EV/PV	Whether the project is behind or ahead of schedule?	SPI > 1 - Ahead of Schedule SPI = 1 – As per Schedule SPI < 1 – Behind schedule
SV	Schedule Variance	SV = EV-PV	How much ahead or behind schedule?	SV > 0 - Ahead of Schedule SV = 0 – As per Schedule SV < 0 – Behind Schedule
CPI	Cost Performance Index	CPI = EV/ AC	Whether the project is within budget	CPI > 1 - Under Spent CPI = 1 – On Budget CPI < 1 – Over Spent
CV	Cost Variance	CV = EV – AC	How much above or below your budget you are	CV > 0 - Under Spent CV = 0 – On Budget CV < 0 – Over Spent
EAC	Estimate at Completion	EAC = BAC/CPI	(Mostly used)	Used if CPI is expected to be same in future
EAC	Estimate at Completion	EAC=AC+BAC–EV		If future work will be accomplished at the planned rate
ETC	Estimate To Complete	ETC = EAC - AC	The expected cost to finish the remaining work	
TCPI	To Complete Performance Index	TCPI= (BAC-EV) / (BAC-AC)	The run rate required to win the match (Run Rate = Spending Rate) (Target Runs = Approved Budget)	TCPI> 1 = Harder to complete the project within approved budget. TCPI <1 = Easier to complete the project within approved budget.

2. PROCESS ITTOS - TABULAR FORMAT

ABBREVIATION USED:

Project Plan	Project Management Plan
OPA	Organizational Process Assets
EEF	Enterprise Environmental Factors
PMIS	Project Management Information System
WPI	Work Performance Information
WPD	Work Performance Data
WPR	Work Performance Report
CRs	Change Requests
PMIS	Project Management Information Systems
Interpersonal Skills	Interpersonal and Team skills
TCPI	To-Complete Performance Index

Process Group

P	Planning
I	Initiating
E	Executing
M&C	Monitoring and Controlling
C	Closing

OPAs and EEFs are input to all the processes.

Project Plan updates and Project Documents Updates are the output of all the processes.

INTEGRATION MANAGEMENT

Process		Inputs	Tools & Techniques	Key Outputs
Develop Project Charter	Initiating	Business Documents Agreements	Expert Judgment Data Gathering Interpersonal Skills Meetings	**Project Charter** Assumption Log
Develop Project Management Plan	Planning	Project Charter Outputs from Other Processes	Expert Judgment Data Gathering Interpersonal Skills Meetings	**Project Management Plan**
Direct & Manage Project Work	Executing	Project Plan Project Documents Approved Change Requests	Expert Judgment Project Management Information Systems (PMIS) Meetings	**Deliverables** Work Performance Data Issue Log Change Requests OPA Updates
Manage Project Knowledge	Executing	Project Plan Project Documents Deliverables	Expert Judgment Knowledge Management Information Management Interpersonal Skills	Lessons Learned Register **OPA Updates**
Monitor & Control Project Work	M&C	Project Plan WPI Agreements	Expert Judgment Data Analysis Decision Making Meetings	**Work Performance Reports** Change Requests
Perform Integrated Change Control	M&C	Project Plan Project Documents Work Performance Reports Change Requests	Expert Judgment Change Control Tools Data Analysis Decision Making Meetings	**Approved Change Requests**
Close Project Or Phase	Closing	Project Charter Project Plan Project Documents Accepted Deliverables Business Documents Agreements Procurement Documents	Expert Judgment Data Analysis Meetings	Project Documents Updates Final Product/Results Transition Final Report **OPA Updates**

2. Process ITTOS - Tabular format

SCOPE MANAGEMENT

Process		Inputs	Tools & Techniques	Key Outputs
Plan Scope Management	Planning	Project Charter Project Plan	Expert Judgment Data Analysis Meetings	**Scope Management Plan** **Requirements Management Plan**
Collect Requirements	Planning	Project Charter Project Plan Project Documents Business Documents Agreements	Expert Judgment Data Gathering Data Analysis Decision Making Data Representation Interpersonal Skills Context Diagrams Prototypes	**Requirements Documentation** **Requirements Traceability Matrix**
Define Scope	Planning	Project Charter Project Plan Project Documents	Expert Judgment Data Analysis Decision Making Interpersonal Skills Product Analysis	**Project Scope Statement**
Create WBS	Planning	Project Plan Project Documents	Expert Judgment Decomposition	**Scope Baseline**
Validate Scope	M&C	Project Plan Project Documents Verified Deliverables WPD	Inspection Decision Making	**Accepted Deliverables** Work Performance Information Change Requests
Control Scope	M&C	Project Plan Project Documents WPD	Data Analysis	**Work Performance Information** Change Requests Project Plan Updates

SCHEDULE MANAGEMENT

Process		Inputs	Tools & Techniques	Key Outputs
Plan Schedule Management	Planning	Project Charter Project Plan	Expert Judgment Data Analysis Meetings	**Schedule Management Plan**
Define Activities	Planning	Project Plan	Expert Judgment Decomposition Rolling Wave Planning Meetings	**Activity List** Activity Attributes **Milestone List** Change Requests
Sequence Activities	Planning	Project Plan Project Documents	Precedence Diagramming Method (PDM) Dependency Determination Leads And Lags PMIS	**Project Schedule NetworkDiagrams (PDM)**
Estimate Activity Durations	Planning	Project Plan Project Documents	Expert Judgment Analogous Estimating Parametric Estimating Three-Point Estimating Bottom-Up Estimating Data Analysis Decision-Making Meetings	**Duration Estimates** Basis of Estimates
Develop Schedule	Planning	Project Plan Project Documents Agreements	Schedule Network Analysis Critical Path Method Resource Optimization Data Analysis Leads And Lags Schedule Compression PMIS Agile Release Planning	**Schedule Baseline** Project Schedule Project Calendars
Control Schedule	M&C	Project Plan Project Documents WPD	Data Analysis Critical Path Method PMIS Resource Optimization Leads and Lags Schedule Compression	**WPI** **Schedule Forecasts** Change Requests

COST MANAGEMENT

Process		Inputs	Tools & Techniques	Key Outputs
Plan Cost Management	Planning	Project Charter Project Plan	Expert Judgment Data Analysis Meetings	**Cost Management Plan**
Estimate Costs	Planning	Project Plan Project Documents	Expert Judgment Analogous Estimating Parametric Estimating Bottom-Up Estimating Three-Point Estimating Data Analysis PMIS Decision Making	**Cost Estimates** Basis of Estimates
Determine Budget	Planning	Project Plan Project Documents Business Documents Agreements	Expert Judgment Cost Aggregation Data Analysis Historical Information Review Funding Limit Reconciliation Financing	**Cost Baseline** Project Funding Requirements
Control Costs	M&C	Project Plan Project Documents Project Funding Requirements WPD	Expert Judgment Data Analysis PMIS TCPI	**WPI** **Cost Forecasts** Change Requests

QUALITY MANAGEMENT

Process		Inputs	Tools & Techniques	Key Outputs
Plan Quality Management	Planning	Project Charter Project Plan Project Documents	Expert Judgment Data Gathering Data Analysis Decision Making Data Representation Test And Inspection Planning Meetings	**Quality Management Plan** **Quality Metrics**
Manage Quality	Executing	Project Plan Project Documents	Data Gathering Data Analysis Decision Making Data Representation Audits Design For X Problem Solving Quality Improvement Methods	**Quality Reports** **Test and Evaluation Documents** Change Requests
Control Quality	M&C	Project Plan Project Documents **Approved Change Requests** Deliverables WPD	Data Gathering Data Analysis Inspections Testing/Product Evaluations Data Representation Meetings	Quality Control Measurements **Verified Deliverables** Work Performance Information Change Requests

RESOURCE MANAGEMENT

Process		Inputs	Tools & Techniques	Key Outputs
Plan Resource Management	Planning	Project Charter Project Plan Project Documents	Expert Judgment Data Representation Organizational Theory Meetings	**Resource Management Plan** **Team Charter**
Estimate Activity Resources	Planning	Project Plan Project Documents	Expert Judgment Bottom-Up Estimating Analogous Estimating Parametric Estimating Data Analysis PMIS Meetings	**Resource Requirements** Basis of Estimates Resource Breakdown Structure
Acquire Resources	Executing	Project Plan Project Documents	Decision-Making Interpersonal Skills Pre-Assignment Virtual Teams	Physical Resource Assignments Project Team Assignments Resource Calendars Change Requests EEF Updates
Develop Team	Executing	Project Plan Project Documents	Co-Location Virtual Teams Communication Technology Interpersonal Skills Recognition And Rewards Trainings Individual & Team Assessment Meetings	**Team Performance Assessment** Change Requests EEF Updates
Manage Team	Executing	Project Plan Project Documents WPR	Interpersonal Skills PMIS	**Change Requests** EEF Updates
Control Resources	M & C	Project Plan Project Documents WPD Agreements	Data Analysis Problem Solving Interpersonal Skills PMIS	WPI Change Requests

COMMUNICATIONS MANAGEMENT

Process		Inputs	Tools & Techniques	Key Outputs
Plan Communications Management	Planning	Project Charter Project Plan Project Documents	Expert Judgment Communication Requirements Analysis Communication Technology Communication Models Communication Methods Interpersonal Skills Data Representation Meetings	**Communications Management Plan**
Manage Communications	Executing	Project Plan Project Documents WPR	Communication Technology Communication Methods Communication Skills PMIS Project Reporting Interpersonal Skills Meetings	**Project Communications** OPA Updates
Monitor Communications	M&C	Project Plan Project Documents WPD	Expert Judgment PMIS Data Analysis Interpersonal Skills Meetings	**Work Performance Information** Change Requests

RISK MANAGEMENT

Process		Inputs	Tools & Techniques	Key Outputs
Plan Risk Management	Planning	Project Charter Project Plan Project Documents	Expert Judgment Data Analysis Meetings	**Risk Management Plan**
Identify Risks	Planning	Project Plan Project Documents Procurement Documents Agreements	Expert Judgment Data Gathering Data Analysis Interpersonal Skills Prompt Lists Meetings	**Risk Register** Risk Report

RISK MANAGEMENT- CONT..

Process		Inputs	Tools & Techniques	Key Outputs
Perform Qualitative Risk Analysis	Planning	Project Plan Project Documents	Expert Judgment Data Gathering Data Analysis Interpersonal Skills Risk Categorization Data Representation Meetings	Project Documents Updates
Perform Quantitative Risk Analysis	Planning	Project Plan Project Documents	Expert Judgment Data Gathering Interpersonal Skills **Representations of Uncertainty** Data Analysis	Project Documents Updates
Plan Risk Responses	Planning	Project Plan Project Documents	Expert Judgment Data Gathering Interpersonal Skills Strategies for Threats Strategies for Opportunities Contingent Response Strategies Strategies-Overall Project Risk Data Analysis Decision Making	**Change Requests** Project Documents Updates
Implement Risk Responses	Executing	Project Plan Project Documents	Expert Judgment Interpersonal Skills PMIS	**Change Requests** Project Documents Updates
Monitor Risks	M&C	Project Plan Project Documents WPD WPR	Data Analysis Audits Meetings	WPI **Change Requests** Project Plan Updates Project Documents Updates OPA Updates

PROCUREMENT MANAGEMENT

Process		Inputs	Tools & Techniques	Key Outputs
Plan Procurement Management	Planning	Project Charter Business Documents Project Plan Project Documents	Expert Judgment Data Gathering Data Analysis Source Selection Analysis Meetings	Procurement Management Plan Procurement Strategy Bid Documents **Procurement Statement of Work** Source Selection Criteria **Make-Or-Buy Decisions** Independent Cost Estimates Change Requests Procurement Documents Updates OPA Updates
Conduct Procurements	Executing	Project Plan Project Documents Procurement Docs Seller Proposals	Expert Judgment **Advertising** **Bidder Conferences** Data Analysis Interpersonal Skills	**Selected Sellers** **Agreements** Change Requests OPA Updates
Control Procurements	M&C	Project Plan Project Documents Agreements Procurement Docs Approved Change Requests WPD	Expert Judgment Claims Administration Data Analysis Inspection Audits	**Closed Procurements** **WPI** Procurement Documentation Updates Change Requests OPA Updates

STAKEHOLDER MANAGEMENT

Process		Inputs	Tools & Techniques	Key Outputs
Identify Stakeholders	Initiating	Project Charter Business Documents Project Plan Project Documents Agreements	Expert Judgment Data Gathering Data Analysis Data Representation Meetings	**Stakeholder Register** Change Requests
Plan Stakeholder Engagement	Planning	Project Charter Project Plan Project Documents Agreements	Expert Judgment Data Gathering Data Analysis Decision Making Data Representation Meetings	**Stakeholder Engagement Plan**
Manage Stakeholder Engagement	Executing	Project Plan Project Documents	Expert Judgment Communication Skills Interpersonal Skills Ground Rules Meetings	**Change Requests**
Monitor Stakeholder Engagement	M&C	Project Plan Project Documents WPD	Data Analysis Decision Making Data Representation Communication Skills Interpersonal Skills Meetings	**WPI** Change Requests

3. PROCESS ITTO - MINDMAPS

PMBOK7 concepts and the PMBOK6 process are kept in mind while designing these mind maps. As a result, the mind maps simplify the process so that you understand the overall concepts.

MIND MAP DESIGN GUIDELINES:

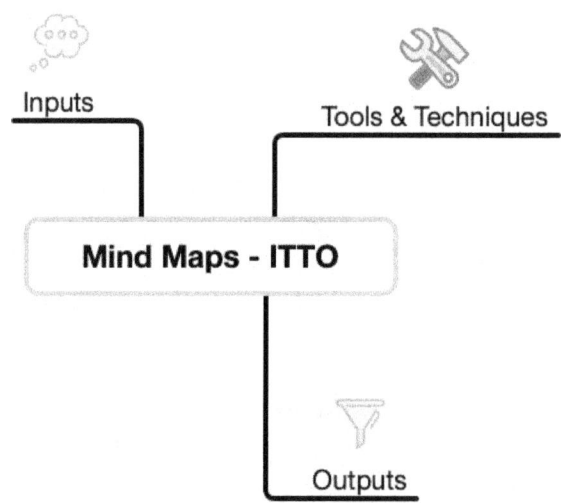

→ The inputs are listed on the left side
→ Tools and Techniques on the right top of the node
→ Output on the right-hand side bottom node
→ The mind maps are simplified to understand concepts
→ PMBOK7 and Agile terms have been added wherever applicable

The text and pictures are interchangeably used, but the conventions are always followed.

INTEGRATION MANAGEMENT

The Integration Management knowledge area focuses on **coordinating project planning**, execution and controlling decisions, and **deciding on the best approach for project success.**

Process Number	Process Name	Process Group
4.1	Develop Project Charter	Initiating
4.2	Develop Project Management Plan	Planning
4.3	Direct & Manage Project Work	Executing
4.4	Manage Project Knowledge	Executing
4.5	Monitor & Control Project Work	Monitoring & Controlling
4.6	Perform Integrated Change Control	Monitoring & Controlling
4.7	Close Project or Phase	Closing

DEVELOP PROJECT CHARTER

Knowledge Area	:	Integration Management
Process Group	:	Initiating
Focus on	:	Developing Charter
Keywords	:	**Formal Authorization of the Project Charter** **Allocation of the Project Manager** **Project announcement in the organization**

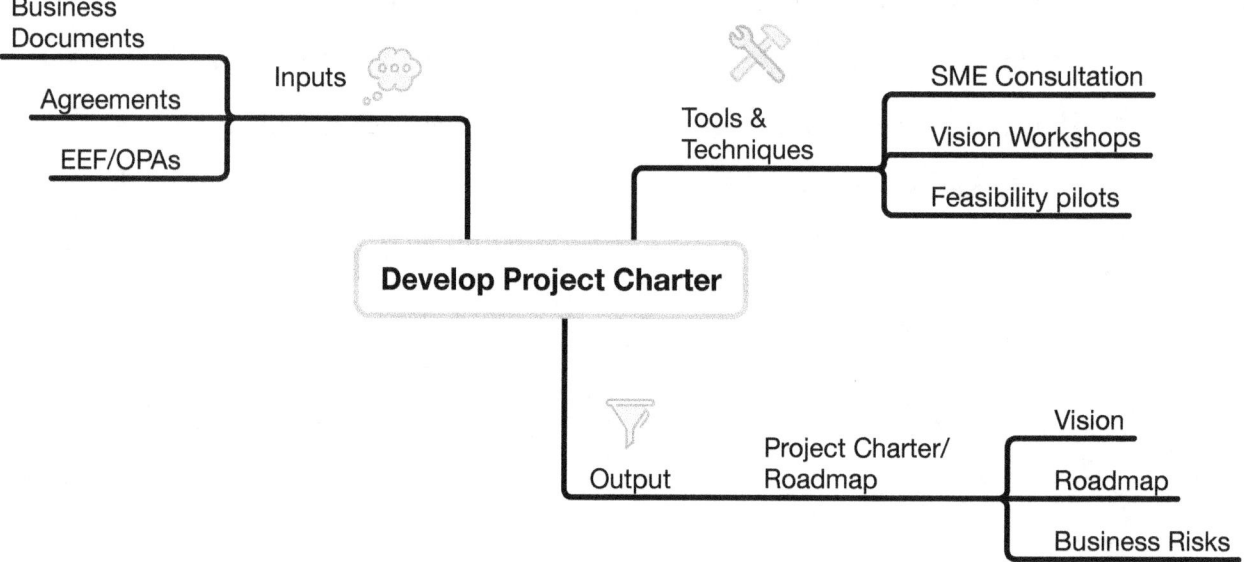

DEVELOP PROJECT MANAGEMENT PLAN

Knowledge Area	:	Integration Management
Process Group	:	Planning
Focus on	:	Creating all the plans and establishing baselines
Keywords	:	**Developing an integrated Project Management Plan** **Subsidiary plans from other Knowledge Areas**

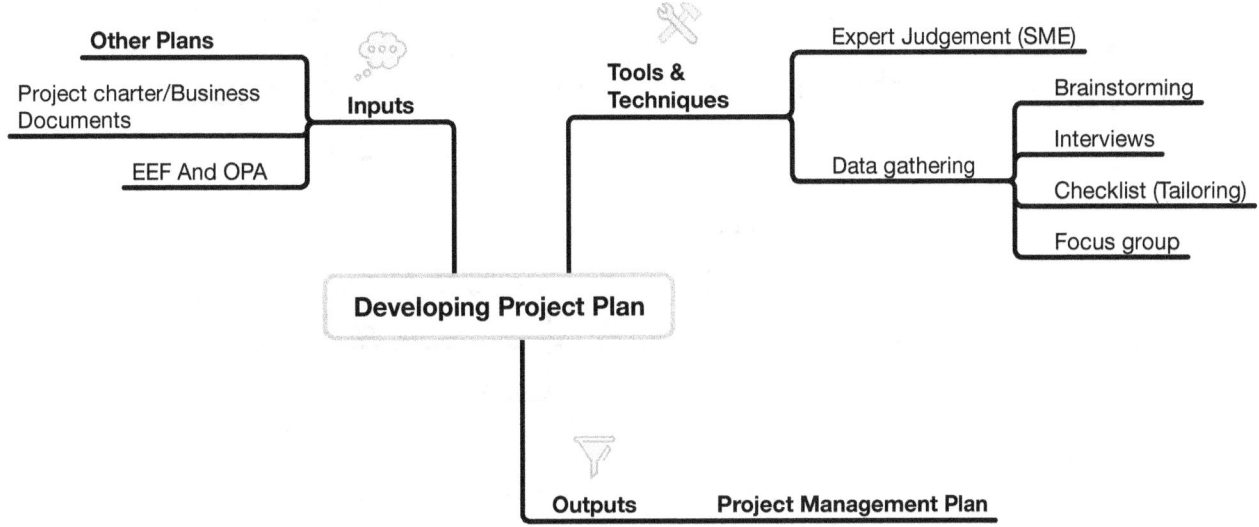

DIRECT AND MANAGE PROJECT WORK

Knowledge Area	:	Integration Management
Process Group	:	Executing
Focus on	:	Deliverables and Work Performance Data
Keywords	:	**Performing the work as per the plan** **Implementing approved changes**

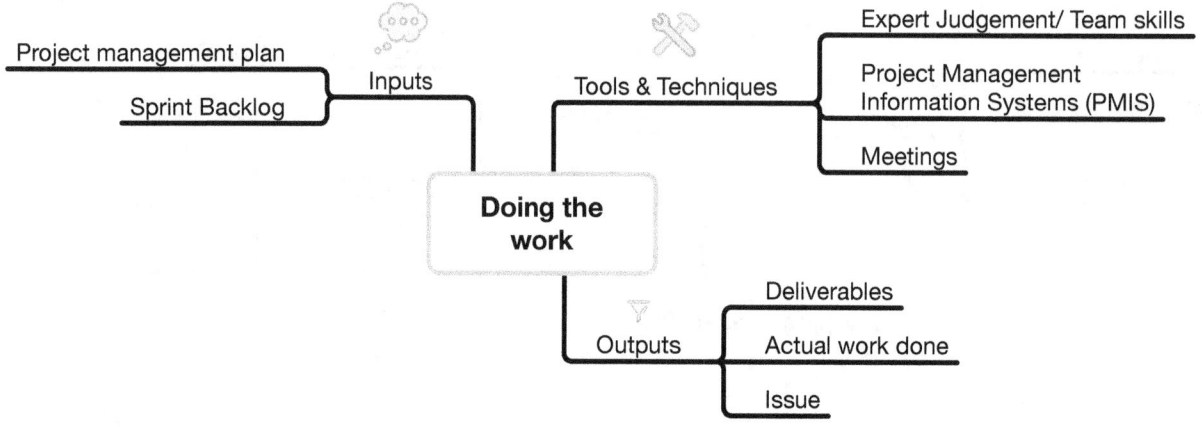

MANAGE PROJECT KNOWLEDGE

Knowledge Area	:	Integration Management
Process Group	:	Executing
Focus on	:	Sharing knowledge
Keywords	:	**Using existing knowledge** **Creating new knowledge**

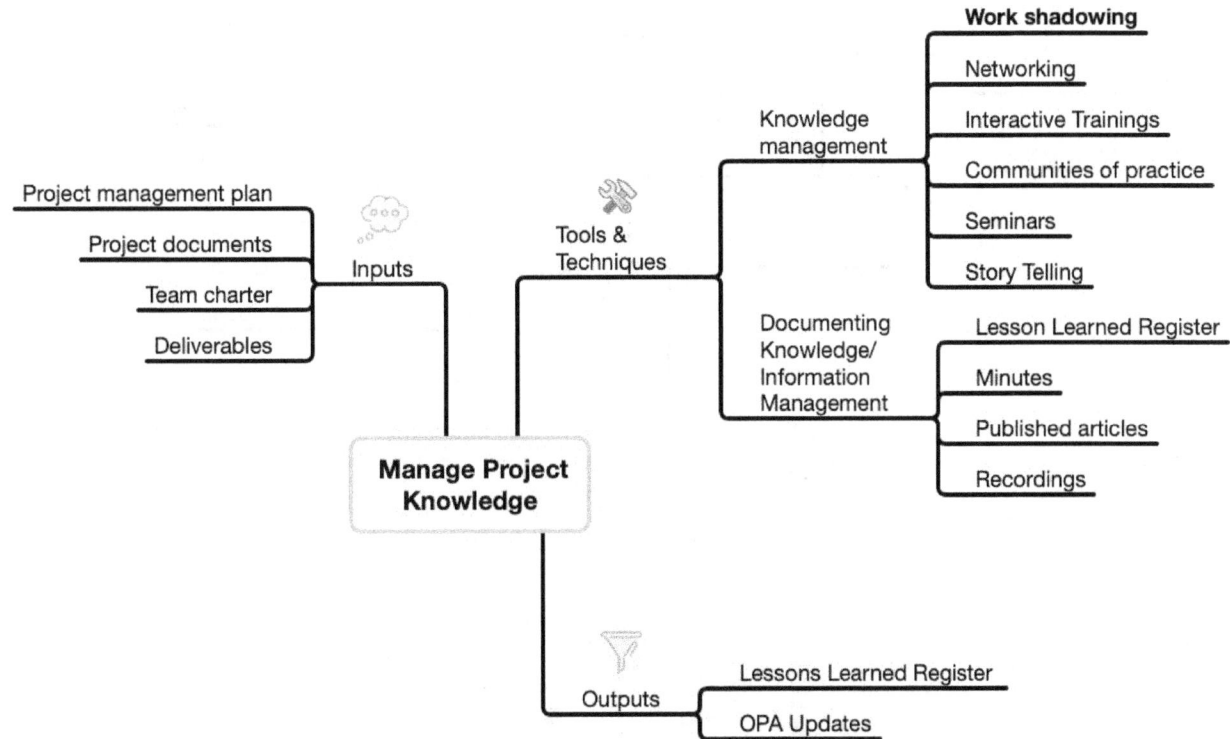

MONITOR & CONTROL PROJECT WORK

Knowledge Area	:	Integration Management
Process Group	:	Monitoring and Controlling
Focus on	:	Status reports and Actions
Keywords	:	**Tracking, reviewing, and reporting progress.** **Forecasts**

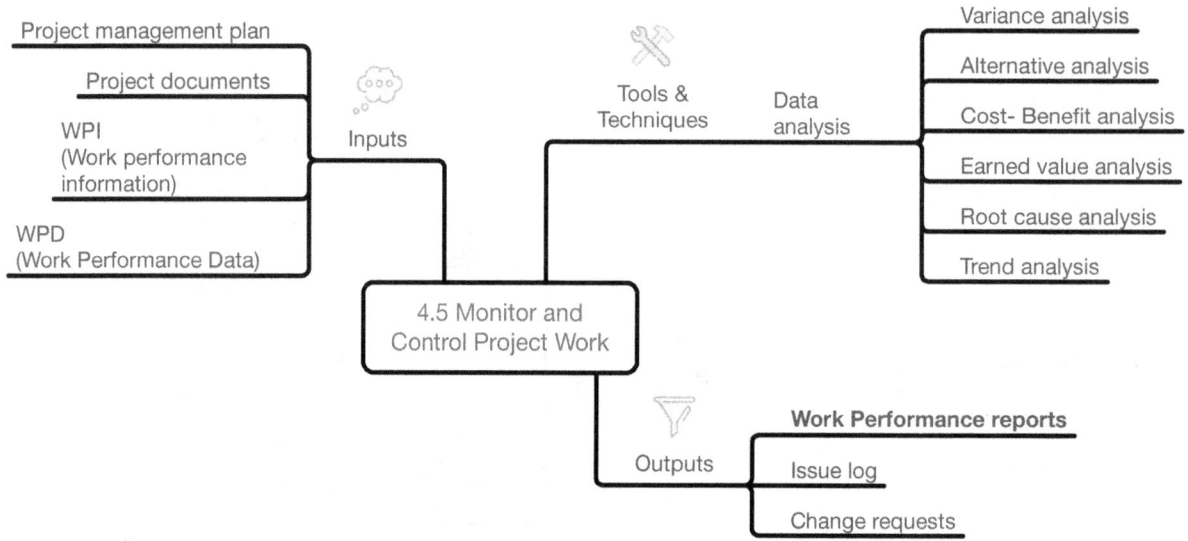

PERFORM INTEGRATED CHANGE CONTROL (PICC/ICC)

Knowledge Area	:	Integration Management
Process Group	:	Monitoring and Controlling
Focus on	:	Change Requests Approval
Keywords	:	**Review of CRs (Change Requests)** **Approval of CRs** **Managing changes**

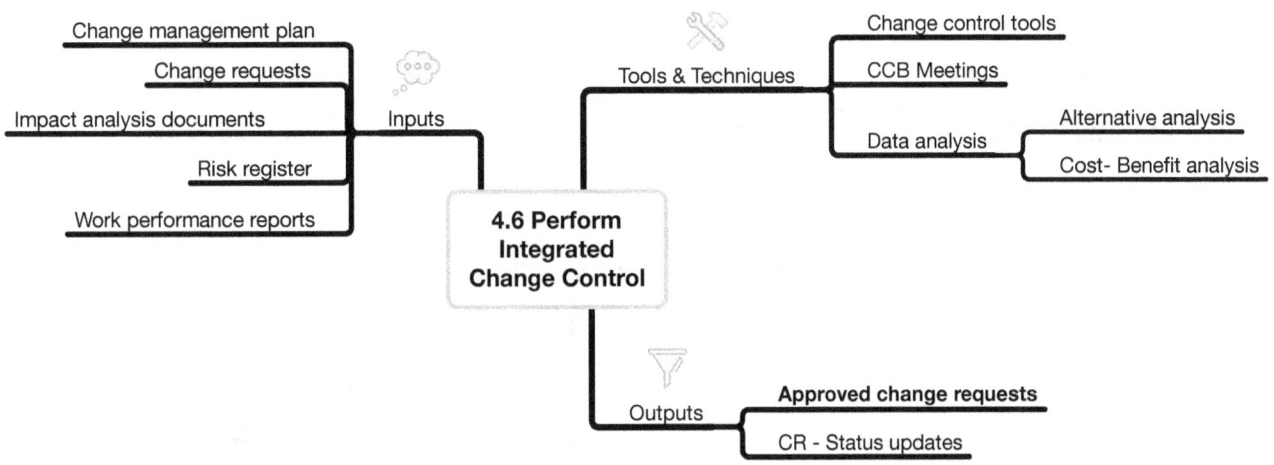

CLOSE PROJECT OR PHASE

Knowledge Area	:	Integration Management
Process Group	:	Closing
Focus on	:	Transition
		Finalizing all activities
Keywords	:	**Administrative closure**

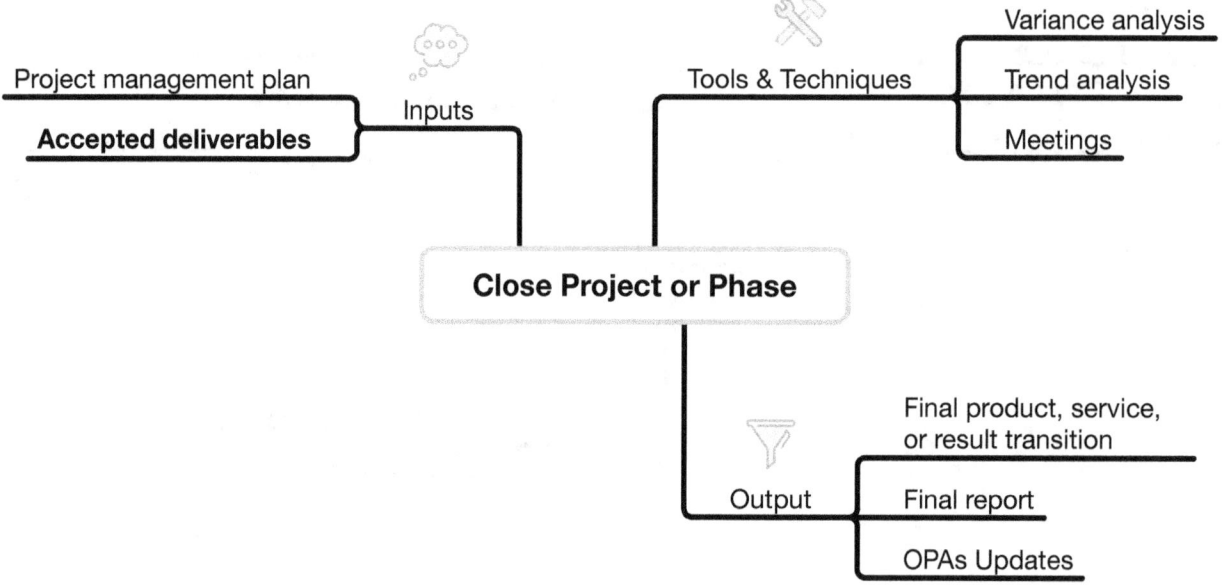

SCOPE MANAGEMENT

Scope Management Knowledge Area includes all the processes to **complete all the work required and only the work required.**

P. No.	Process Name	Process Group
5.1	Plan Scope Management	Planning
5.2	Collect Requirements	Planning
5.3	Define Scope	Planning
5.4	Create WBS	Planning
5.5	Validate Scope	Monitoring & controlling
5.6	Control Scope	Monitoring & controlling

PLAN SCOPE MANAGEMENT

Knowledge Area	:	Scope Management
Process Group	:	Planning
Focus on	:	Developing Requirements and Scope Management Plan
Keywords	:	**Developing criteria to define and validate requirements**
		Developing criteria to define and validate scope

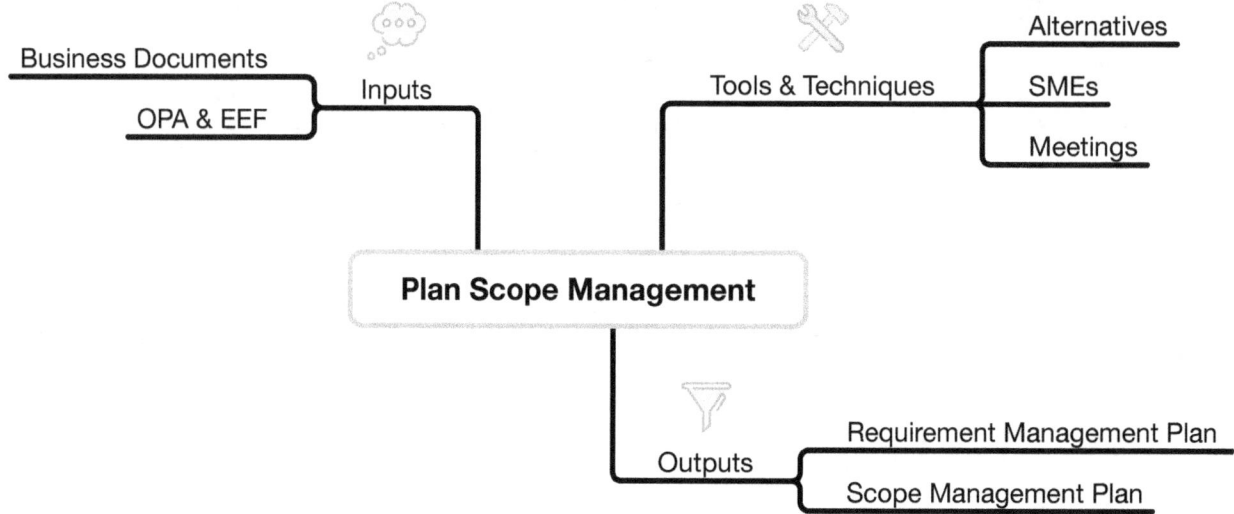

COLLECT REQUIREMENTS

Knowledge Area	:	Scope Management
Process Group	:	Planning
Focus on	:	Getting and documenting requirements.
Keywords	:	**Determining and documenting stakeholders' needs and requirements. Establishing the mechanism to cross-verify the deliverables**

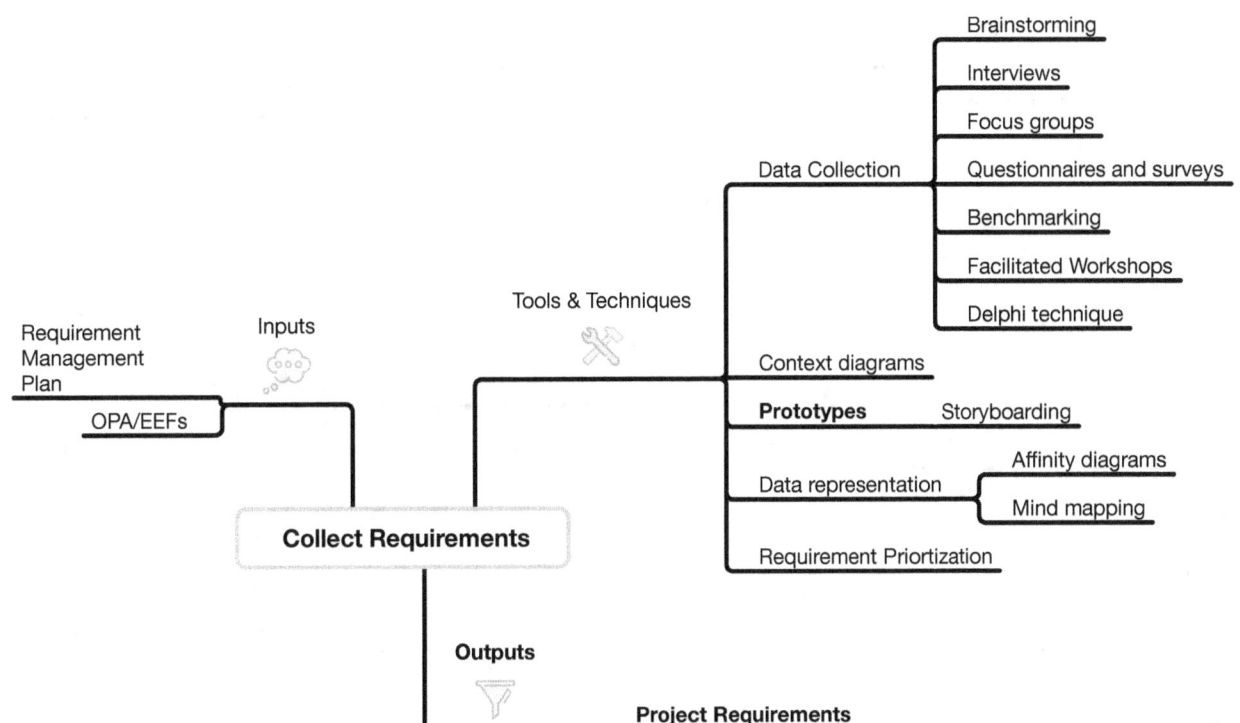

DEFINE SCOPE

Knowledge Area	:	Scope Management
Process Group	:	Planning
Focus on	:	Product and Project Scope
Keywords	:	**A detailed description of the product and project.** **In-scope, out-of-scope, assumptions and constraint**

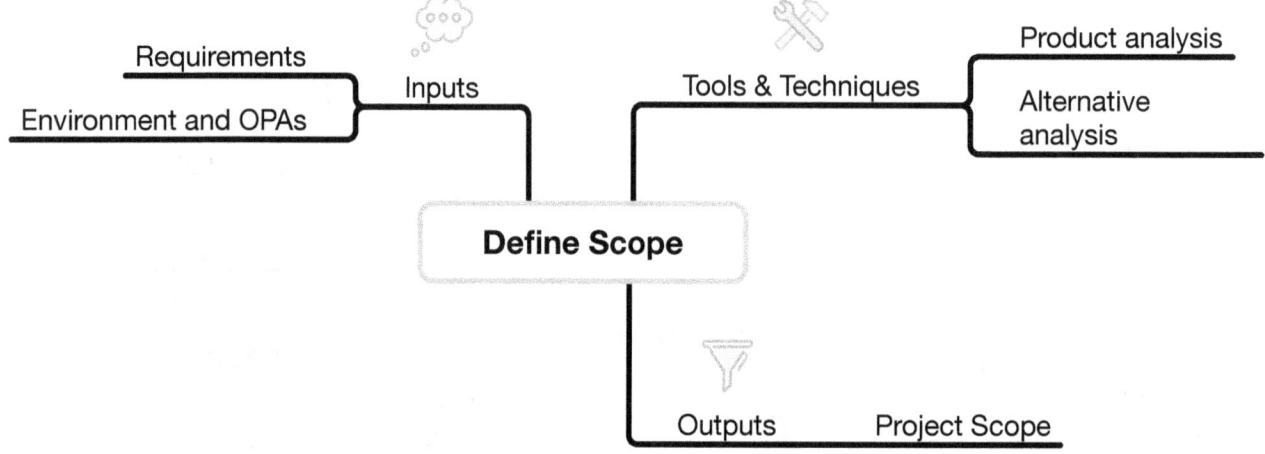

CREATE WORK BREAKDOWN STRUCTURE (WBS)

Knowledge Area	:	Scope Management
Process Group	:	Planning
Focus on	:	Creating a WBS and scope baseline
Keywords	:	**Subdividing project work into smaller, manageable units**

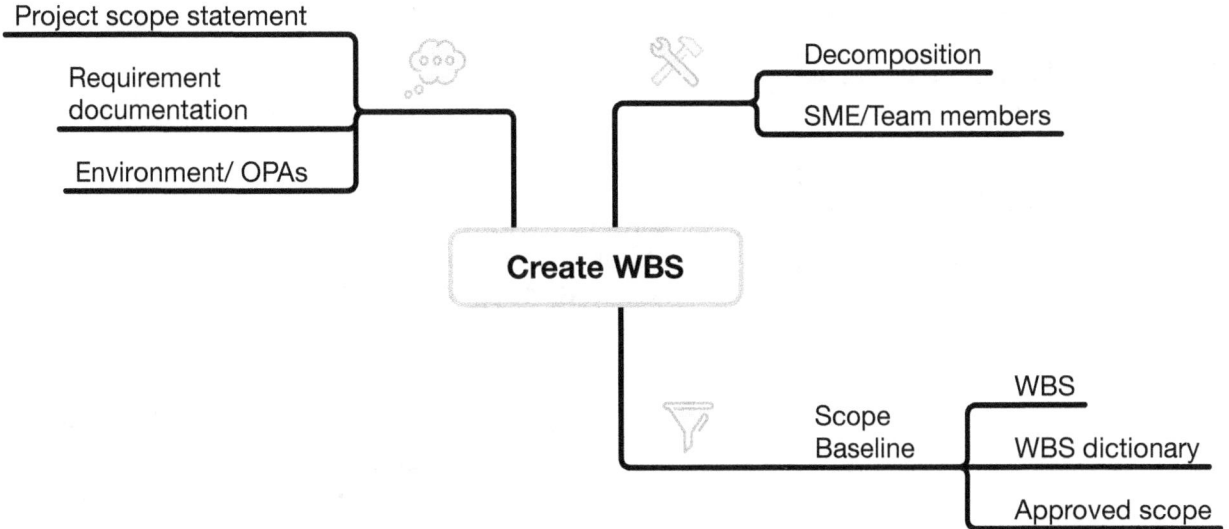

VALIDATE SCOPE

Knowledge Area	:	Scope Management
Process Group	:	Monitoring and controlling
Focus on	:	Customer acceptance of deliverables
Keywords	:	**Formalizing acceptance of the completed deliverables**

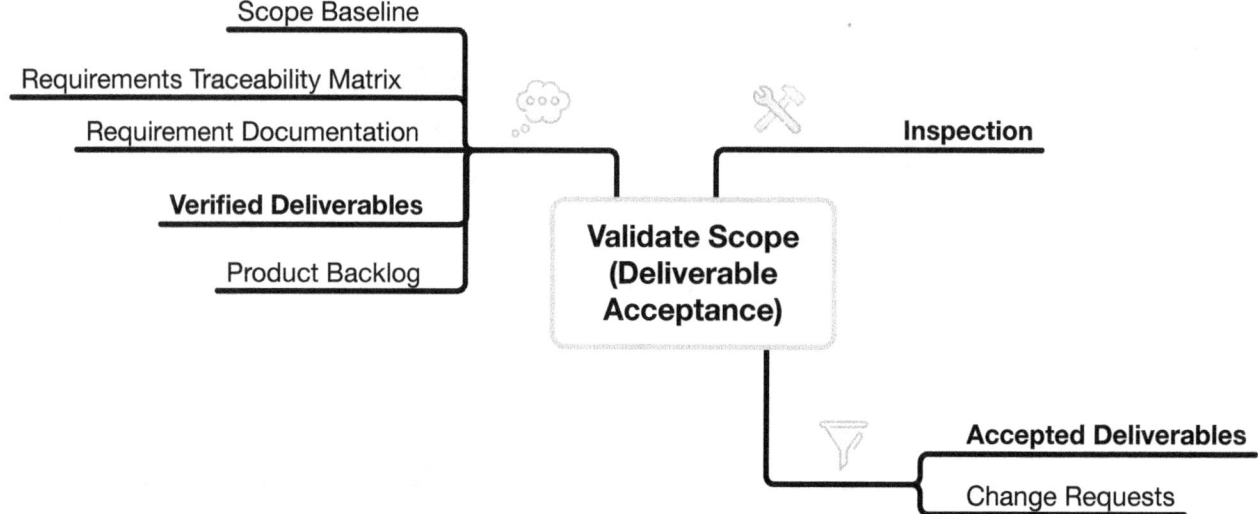

CONTROL SCOPE

Knowledge Area	:	Scope Management
Process Group	:	Monitoring and Controlling
Focus on	:	Scope Variance and action
Keywords	:	**Managing changes to the Scope Baseline** **Understanding scope variance** **Taking action**

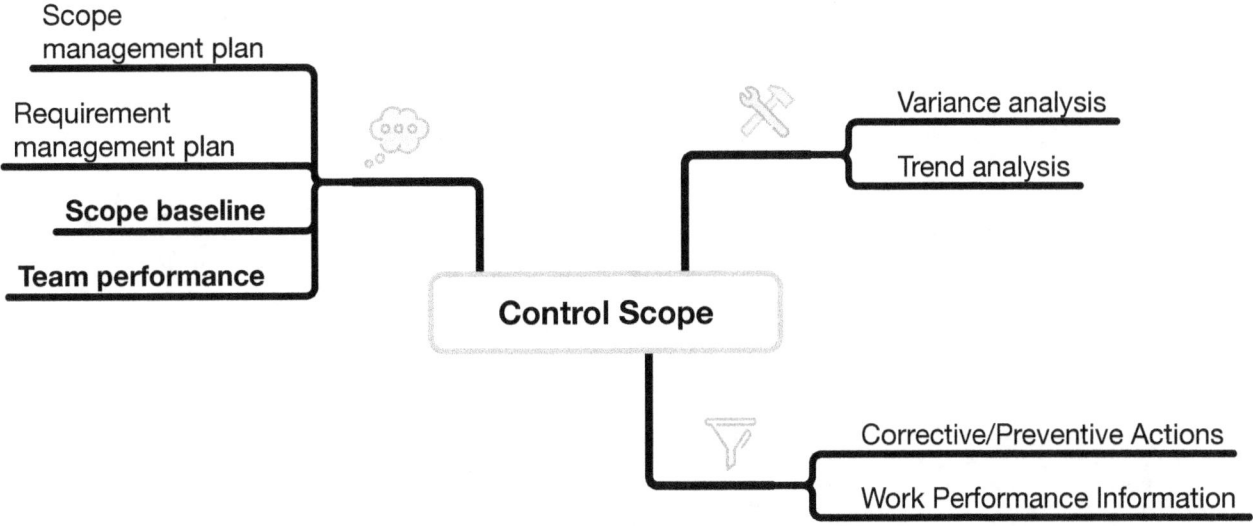

SCHEDULE MANAGEMENT

Project Schedule Management is to estimate and control the schedule to **complete ON TIME**.

Process No.	Process Name	Process Group
6.1	Plan Schedule Management	Planning
6.2	Define Activities	Planning
6.3	Sequence Activities	Planning
6.4	Estimate Activity Durations	Planning
6.5	Develop Schedule	Planning
6.6	Control Schedule	Monitoring & Controlling

PLAN SCHEDULE MANAGEMENT

Knowledge Area	:	Schedule Management
Process Group	:	Planning
Focus on	:	Developing Schedule Management Plan
Keywords	:	**Establishing the policies, procedures**
		Developing and controlling the Project Schedule

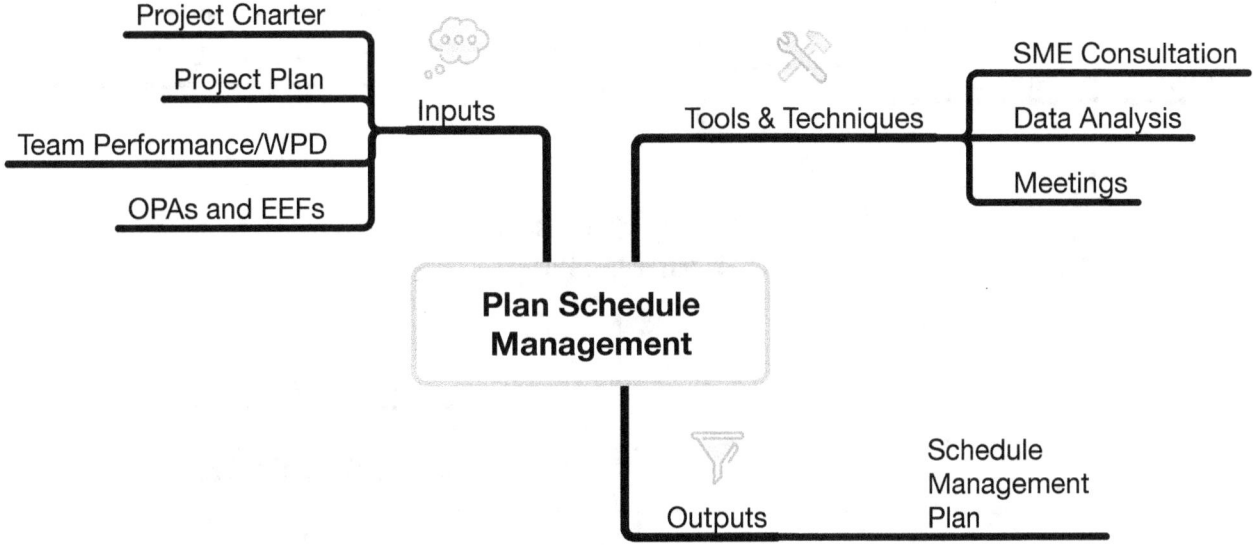

DEFINE ACTIVITIES

Knowledge Area	:	Schedule Management
Process Group	:	Planning
Focus on	:	Activities and Milestone list
Keywords	:	**Actions to be performed to produce project deliverables. Starts from WBS**

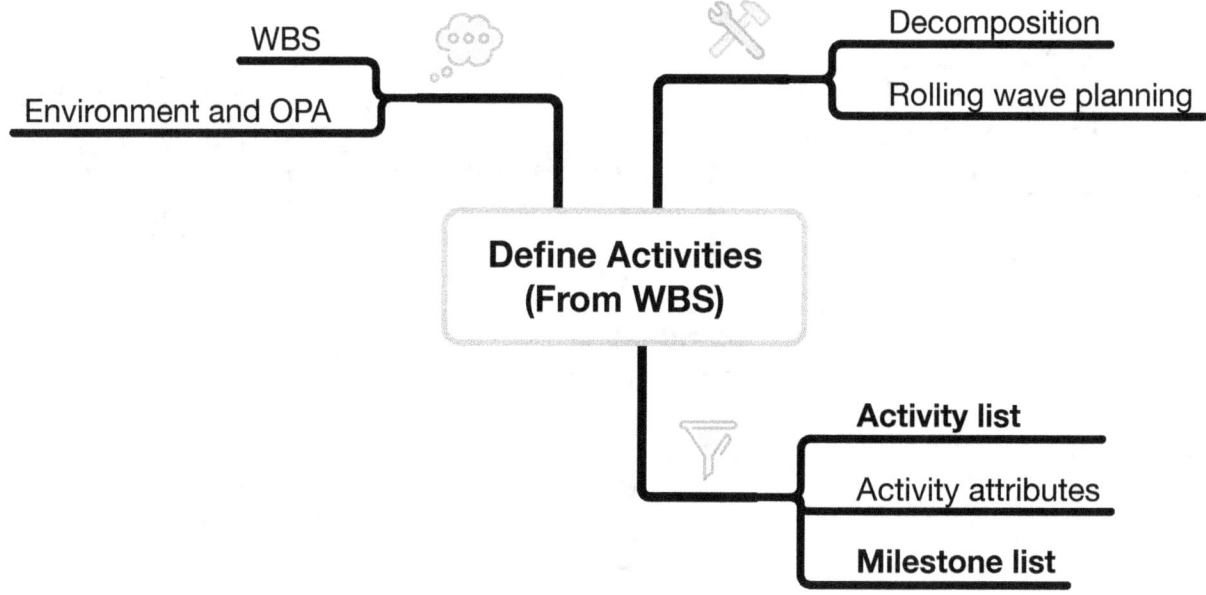

SEQUENCE ACTIVITIES

Knowledge Area	:	Schedule Management
Process Group	:	Planning
Focus on	:	Activity relationship
Keywords	:	**Identifying relationships amongst activities**
		Shown using Activity on Node (AON), referred to as PDM

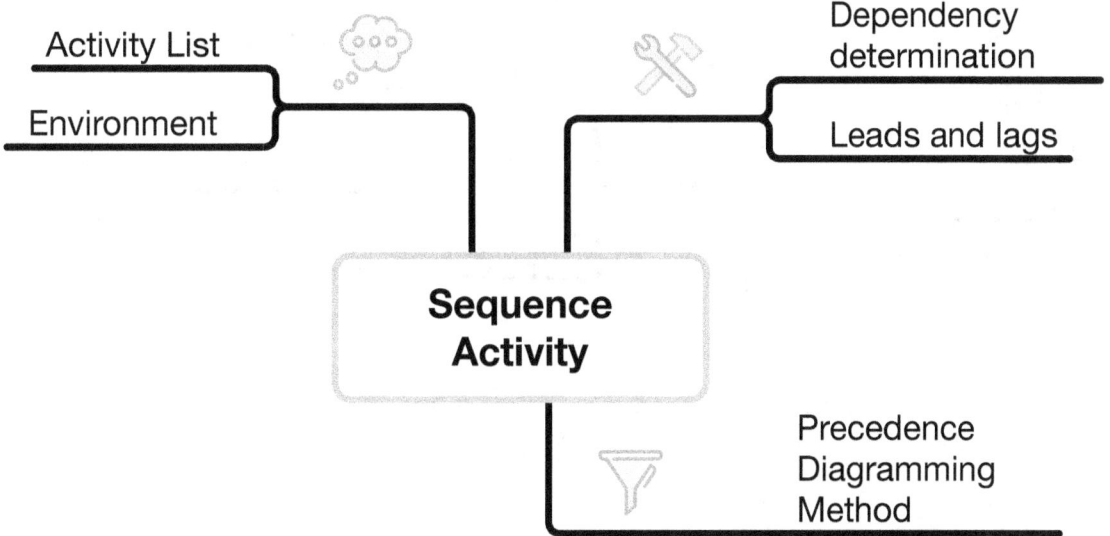

ESTIMATE ACTIVITY DURATIONS

Knowledge Area	:	Schedule Management
Process Group	:	Planning
Focus on	:	Estimation techniques
Keywords	:	**Estimating the number of work periods**

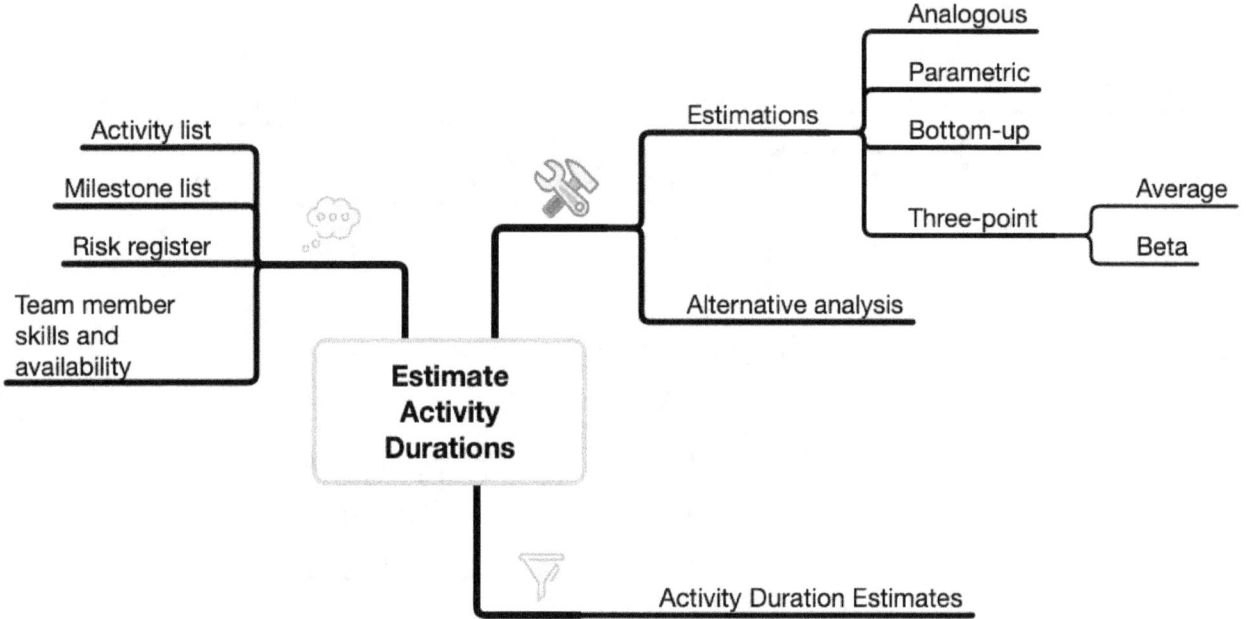

DEVELOP SCHEDULE

Knowledge Area	:	Schedule Management
Process Group	:	Planning
Focus on	:	Developing Schedule
Keywords	:	**Analyzing activity sequences, durations** **Apply Schedule Constraints** **Project Schedule Baseline**

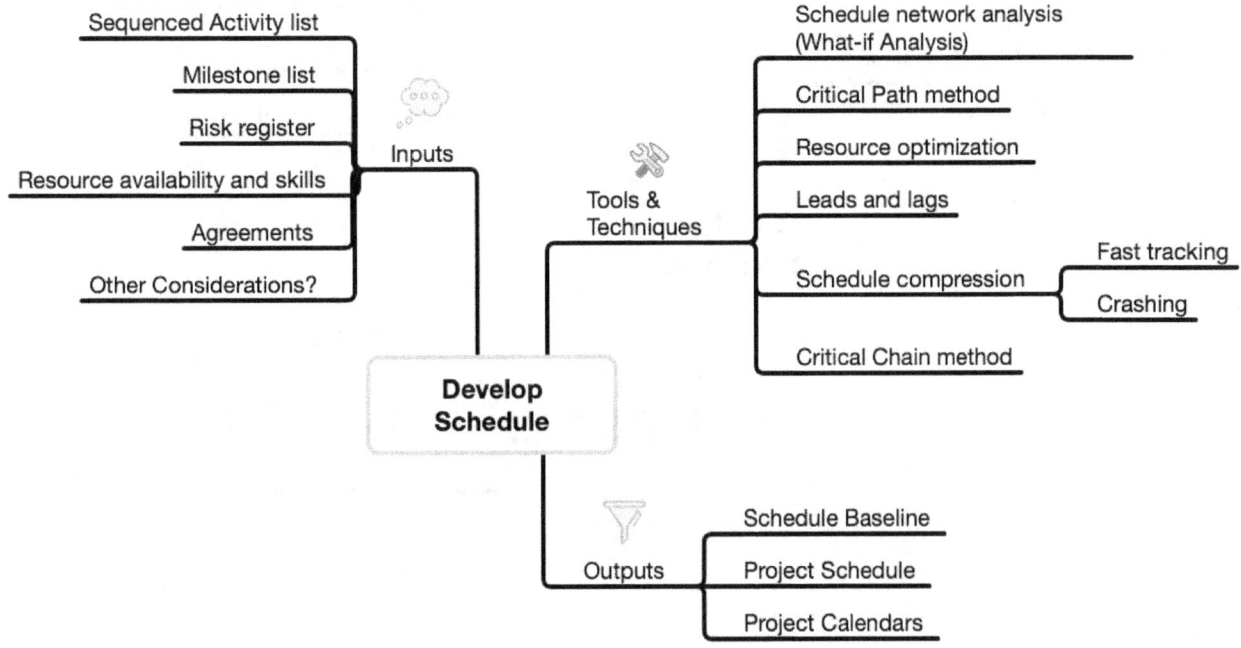

CONTROL SCHEDULE

Knowledge Area	:	Schedule Management
Process Group	:	Monitoring and controlling
Focus on	:	Variance Analysis to arrive at WPI for schedule
Keywords	:	**Analyze planned vs. actual schedule**
		Taking action

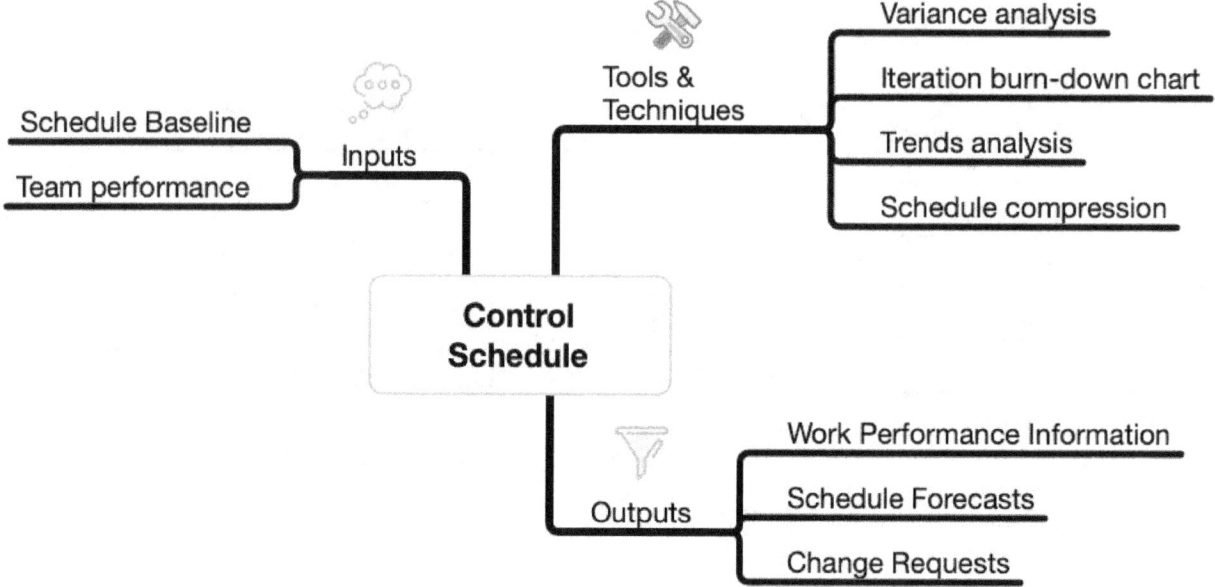

COST MANAGEMENT

Planning, estimating, and controlling costs to complete the project **within budget**.

No	Process Name	Process Group
7.1	Plan Cost Management	Planning
7.2	Estimate Costs	Planning
7.3	Determine Budget	Planning
7.4	Control Costs	Monitoring & controlling

PLAN COST MANAGEMENT

Knowledge Area	:	Cost Management
Process Group	:	Planning
Focus on	:	Cost Management Plan
Keywords	:	**Defining how costs will be estimated and controlled**

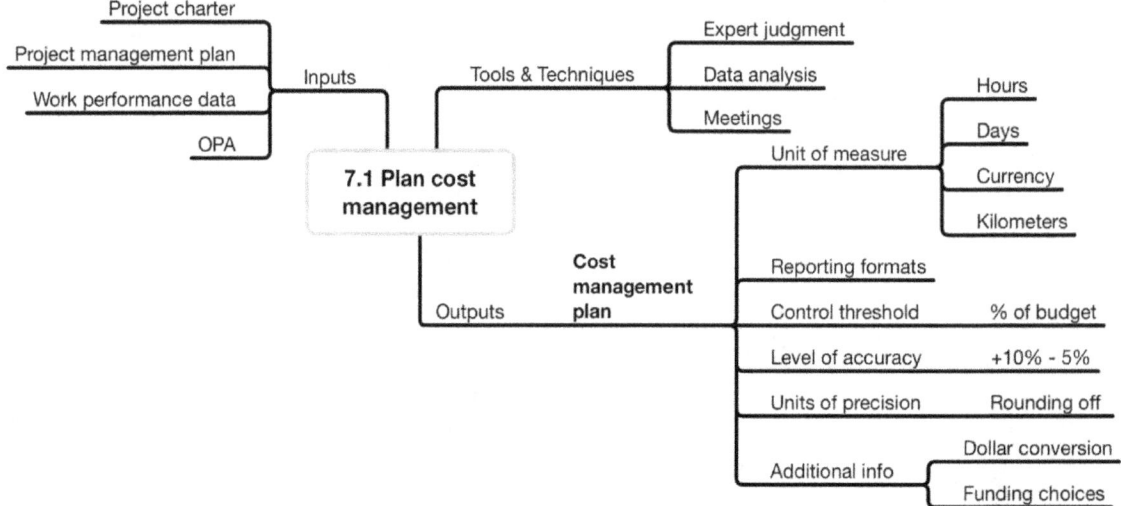

ESTIMATE COSTS

Knowledge Area	:	Cost Management
Process Group	:	Planning
Focus on	:	Cost Management Plan
Keywords	:	**Defining how costs will be estimated and controlled**

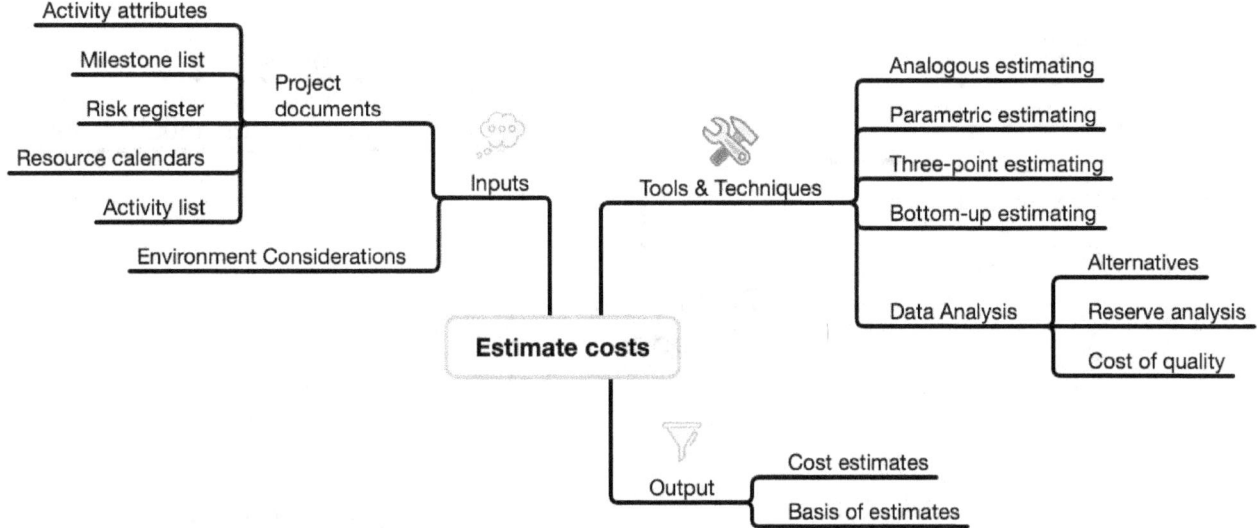

DETERMINE BUDGET

Knowledge Area	:	Cost Management
Process Group	:	Planning
Focus on	:	Cost Management Plan
Keywords	:	**Arriving at the approved budget**

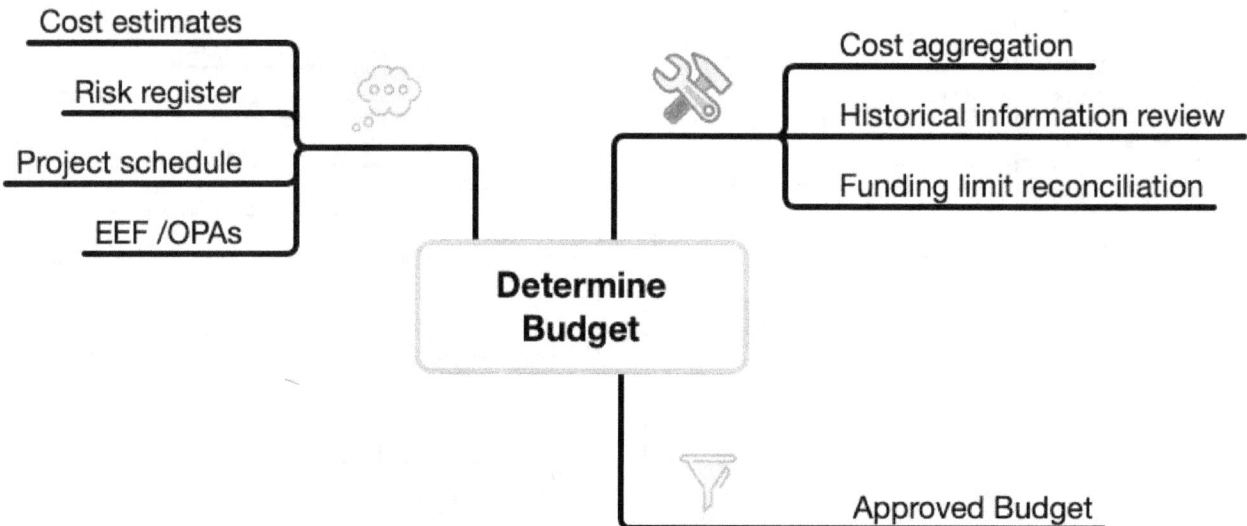

CONTROL COSTS

Knowledge Area	:	Cost Management
Process Group	:	Monitoring and Controlling
Focus on	:	Cost Management Plan
Keywords	:	**Planned vs. actual cost spend and action**

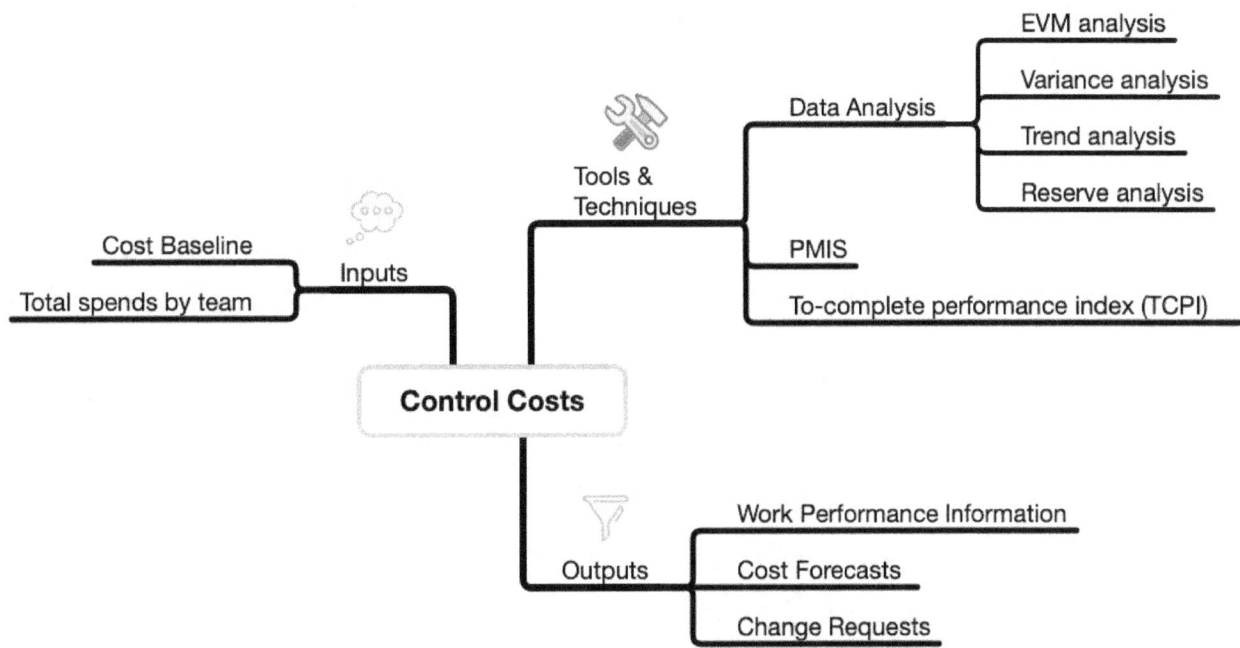

QUALITY MANAGEMENT

It includes the processes and activities of the **performing organization** that determines **quality policies, objectives**, and responsibilities so that the project will **satisfy its undertaken needs.**

No	Process Name	Process Group
8.1	Plan Quality Management	Planning
8.2	Manage Quality	Executing
8.3	Control Quality	Monitoring & Controlling

PLAN QUALITY MANAGEMENT

Knowledge Area	:	Quality Management
Process Group	:	Planning
Focus on	:	Quality requirements & standards
Keywords	:	**Identifying quality requirements & standards** **Tailoring Processes**

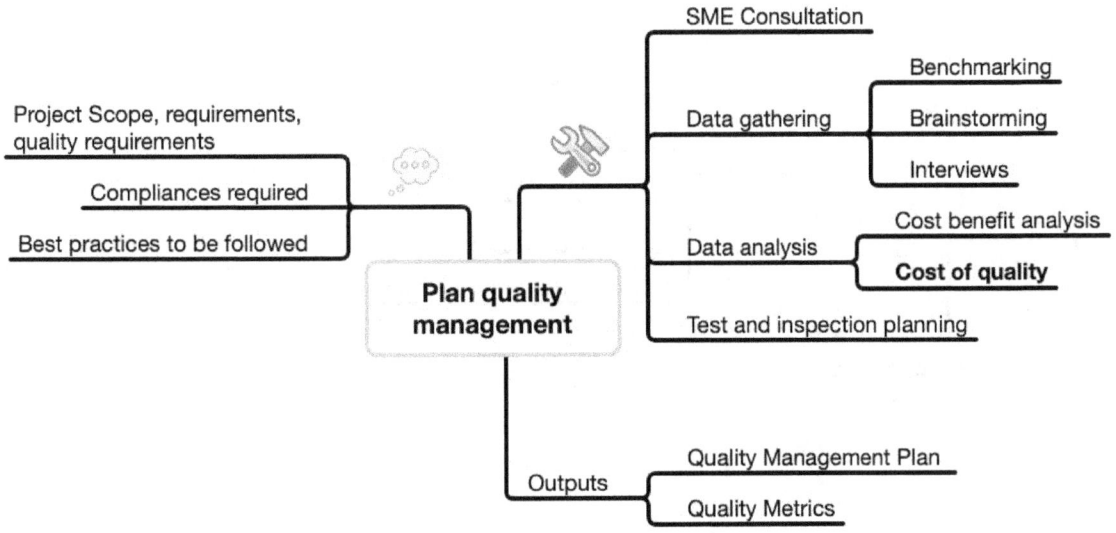

MANAGE QUALITY

Knowledge Area	:	Quality Management
Process Group	:	Planning
Focus on	:	Audits
Keywords	:	Implementing the Quality Plan Auditing Preventing defects.

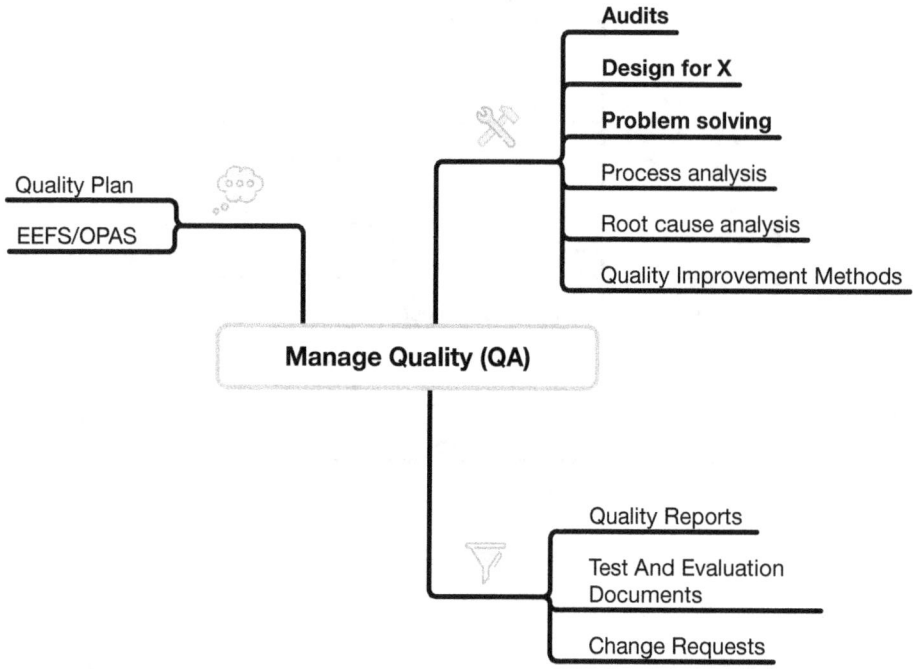

3. Process ITTO - Mindmaps
CONTROL QUALITY

Knowledge Area	:	Quality Management
Process Group	:	Planning
Focus on	:	Product Testing
Keywords	:	**Testing the deliverables**
		Project deliverables meet customer expectations

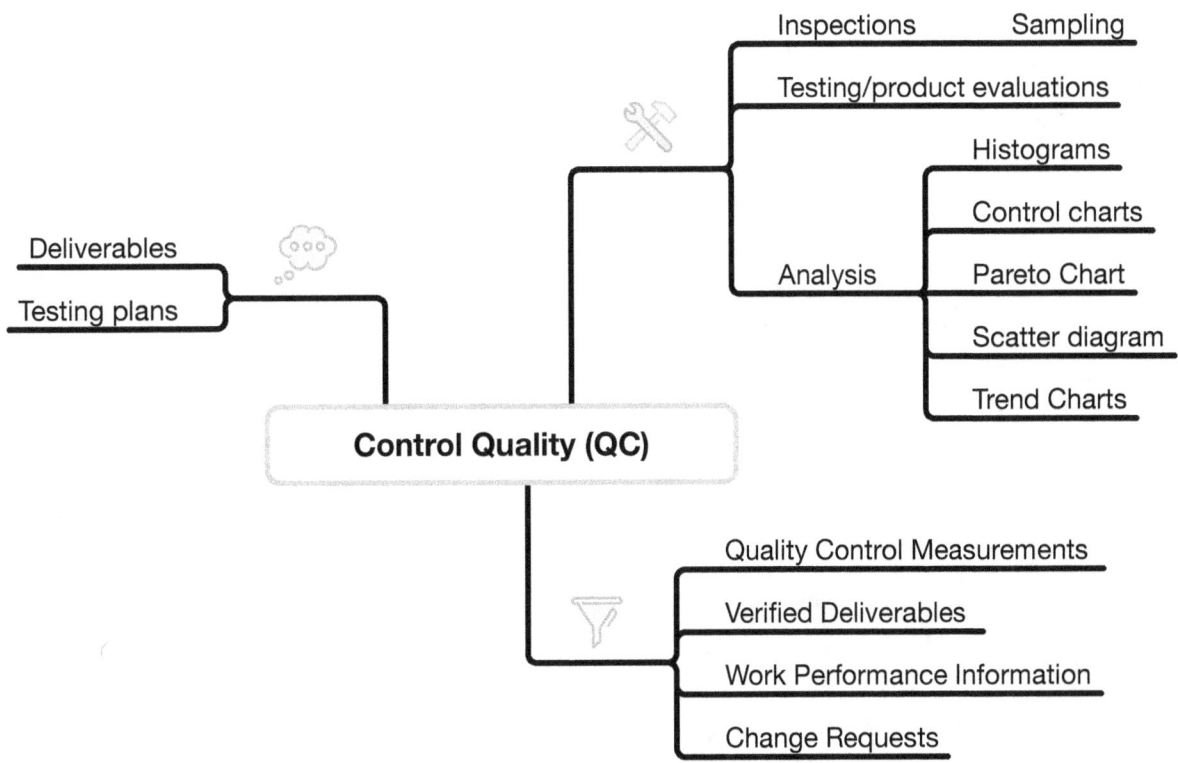

51

RESOURCE MANAGEMENT

Planning, acquiring and managing resources to complete the project.

No	Process Name	Process Group
9.1	Plan Resource Management	Planning
9.2	Estimate Activity Resources	Planning
9.3	Acquire Resources	Executing
9.4	Develop Team	Executing
9.5	Manage Team	Executing
9.6	Control Resources	Monitoring & Controlling

PLAN RESOURCE MANAGEMENT

Knowledge Area	:	Resource Management
Process Group	:	Planning
Focus on	:	Creating resource plan
Keywords	:	**Documenting resource plan** **Reporting relationships, Rewards** **Physical resource plan**

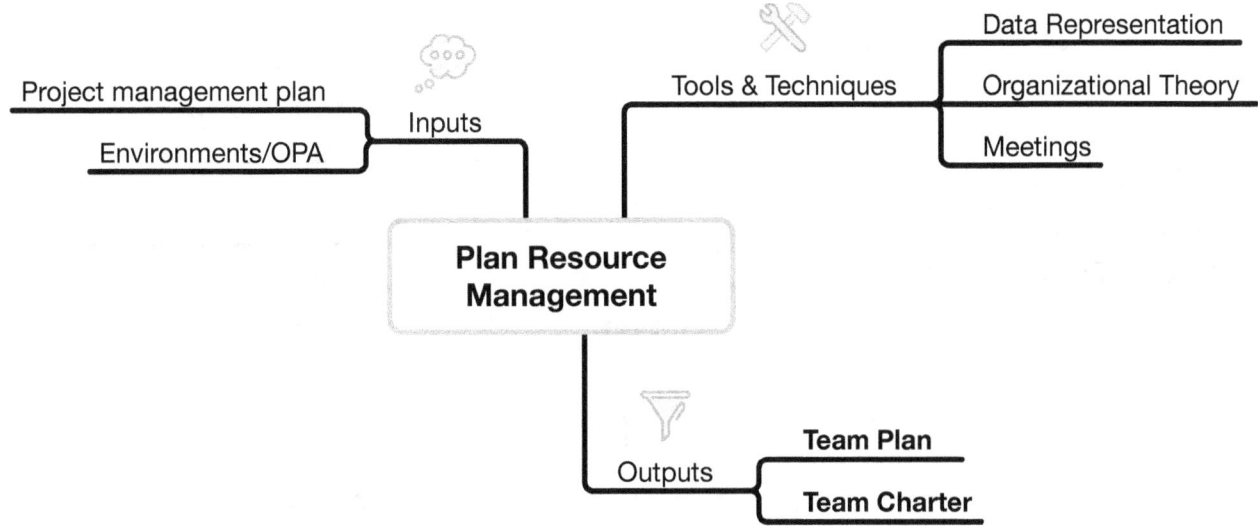

ESTIMATE ACTIVITY RESOURCES

Knowledge Area	:	Resource Management
Process Group	:	Planning
Focus on	:	Resource Estimation
Keywords	:	**Estimating Team resources**
		Type and quantities of the resource.

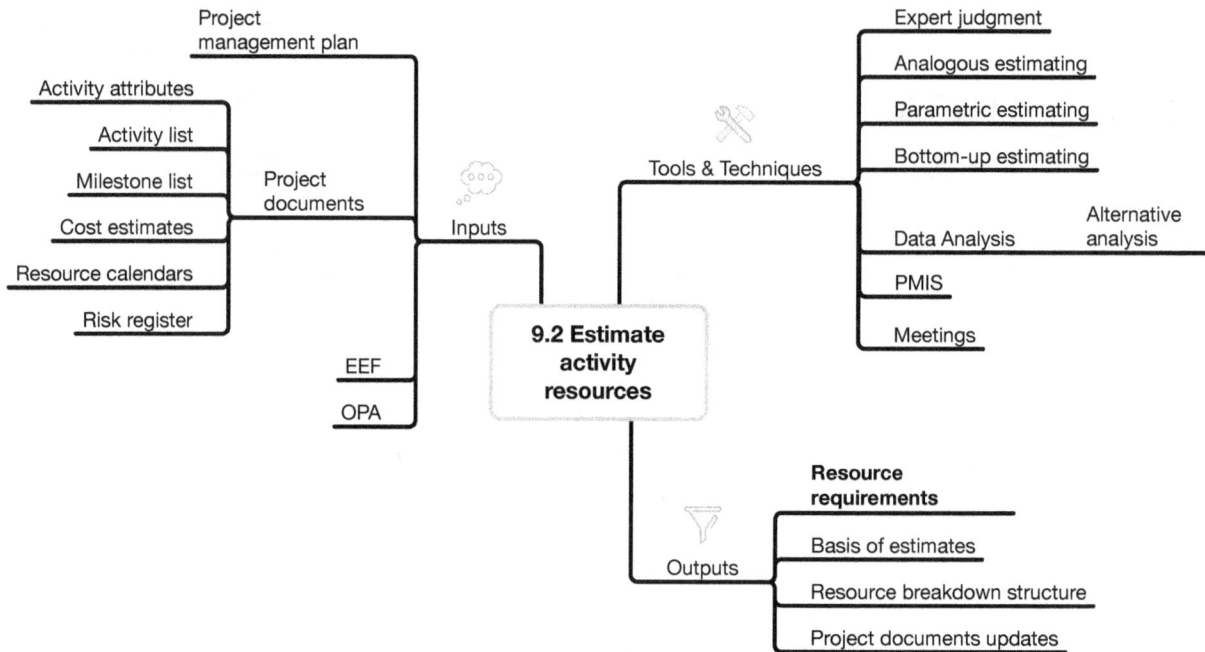

ACQUIRE RESOURCES

Knowledge Area	:	Resource Management
Process Group	:	Executing
Focus on	:	On-boarding resources (both physical and team)
Keywords	:	**Confirming equipment, team members** **Team selection**

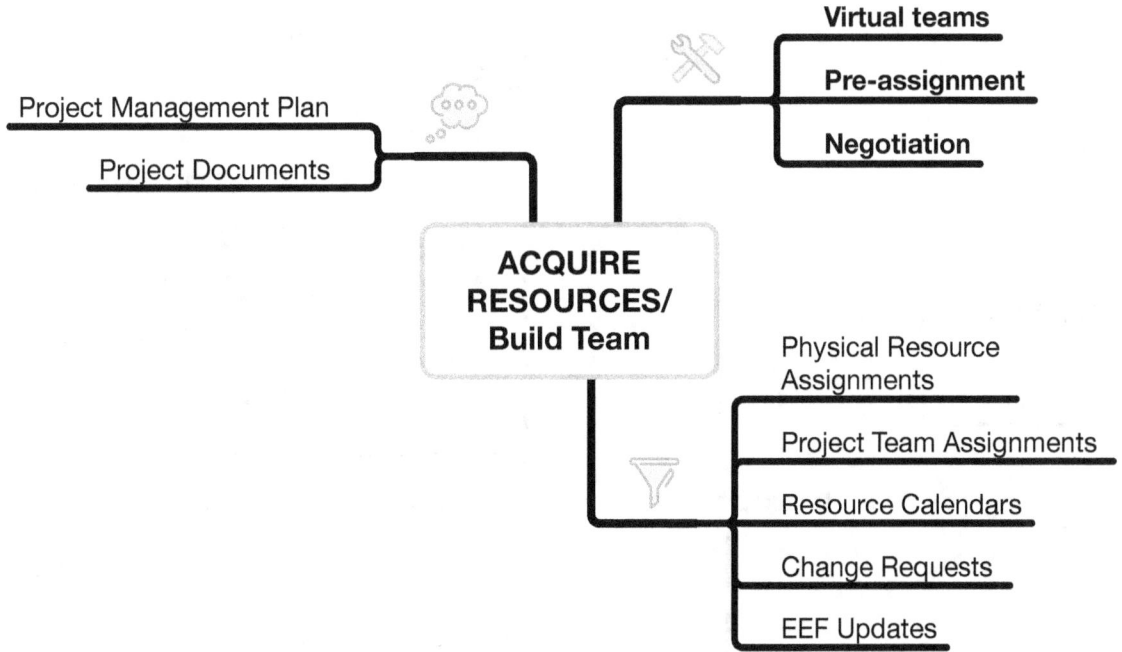

DEVELOP TEAM

Knowledge Area	:	Resource Management
Process Group	:	Executing
Focus on	:	Assessing and improving team productivity
Keywords	:	**Improving competencies and team member interactions** **Improve overall team productivity**

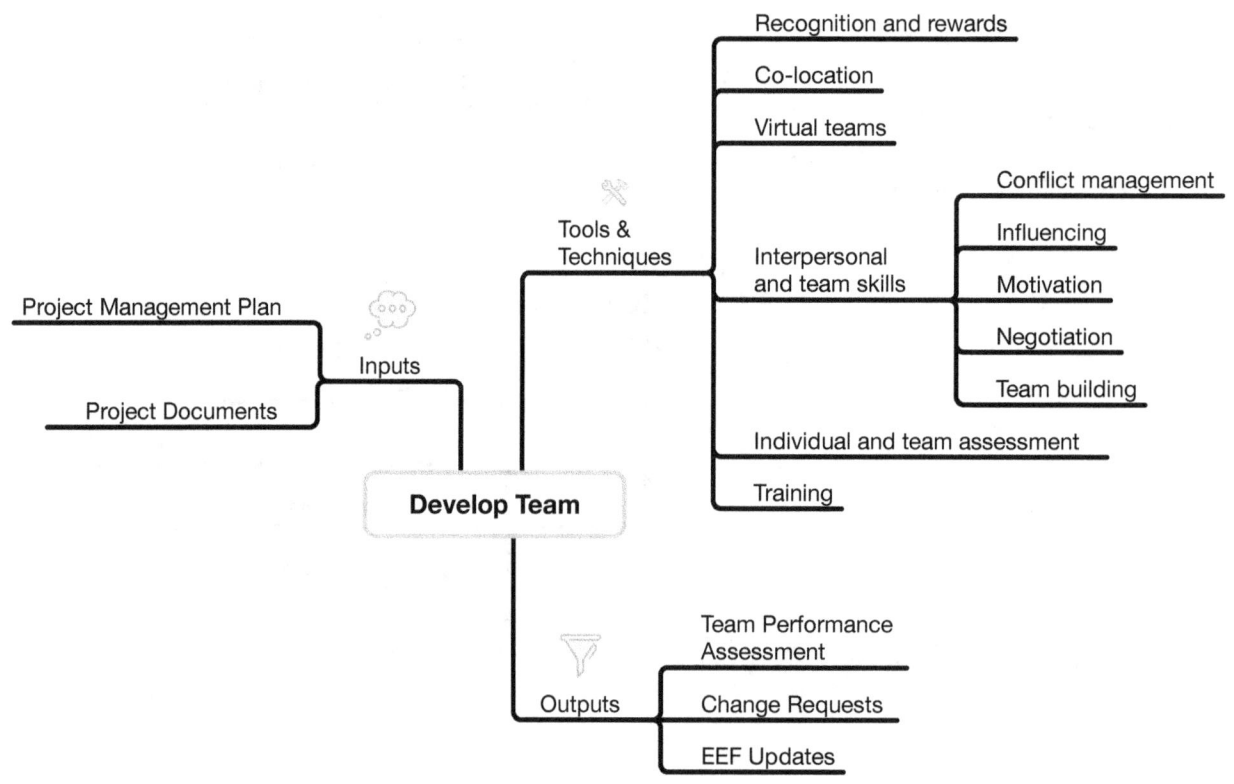

MANAGE TEAM

Knowledge Area	:	Resource Management
Process Group	:	Executing
Focus on	:	Sustaining team performance
Keywords	:	**Providing feedback** **Resolving issues** **Optimizing team performance**

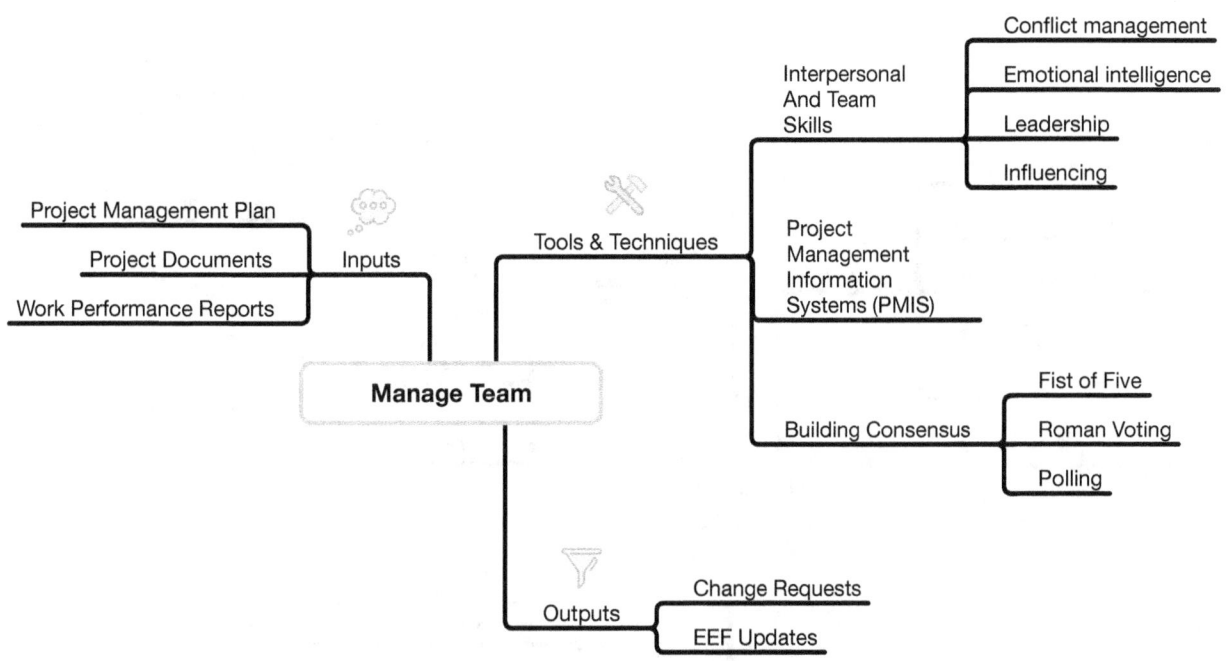

CONTROL RESOURCES

Knowledge Area	:	Resource Management
Process Group	:	Monitoring and Controlling
Focus on	:	Resource utilization
Keywords	:	**Variance analysis** **Ensuring availability of physical resources** **Optimizing resource utilization**

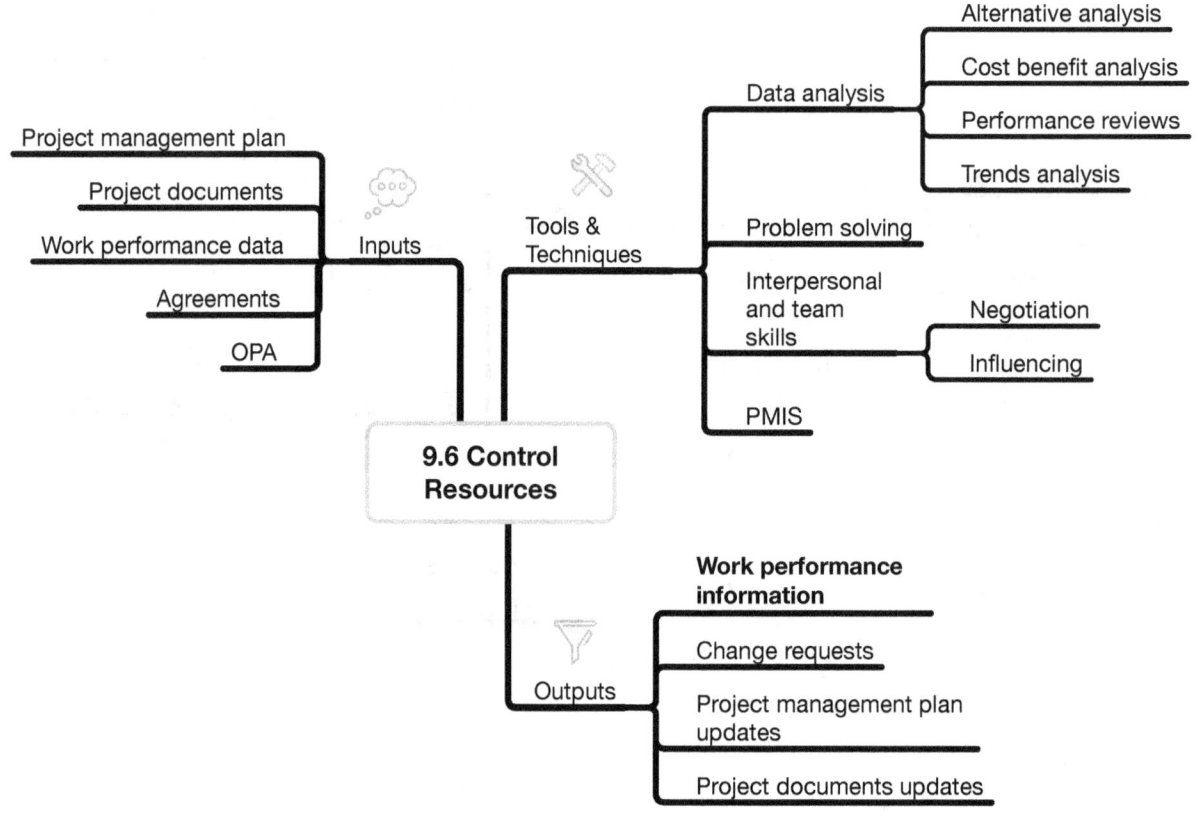

COMMUNICATIONS MANAGEMENT

Project Communication Management focuses on developing and communicating artifacts that facilitate **effective information exchange** with project stakeholders.

No	Process Name	Process Group
10.1	Plan Communications Management	Planning
10.2	Manage Communications	Executing
10.3	Monitor Communications	Monitoring & Controlling

PLAN COMMUNICATIONS MANAGEMENT

Knowledge Area	:	Communications Management
Process Group	:	Planning
Focus on	:	Planning meetings and information distribution plan
Keywords	:	**Developing an appropriate communication approach** **Based on stakeholders' information needs**

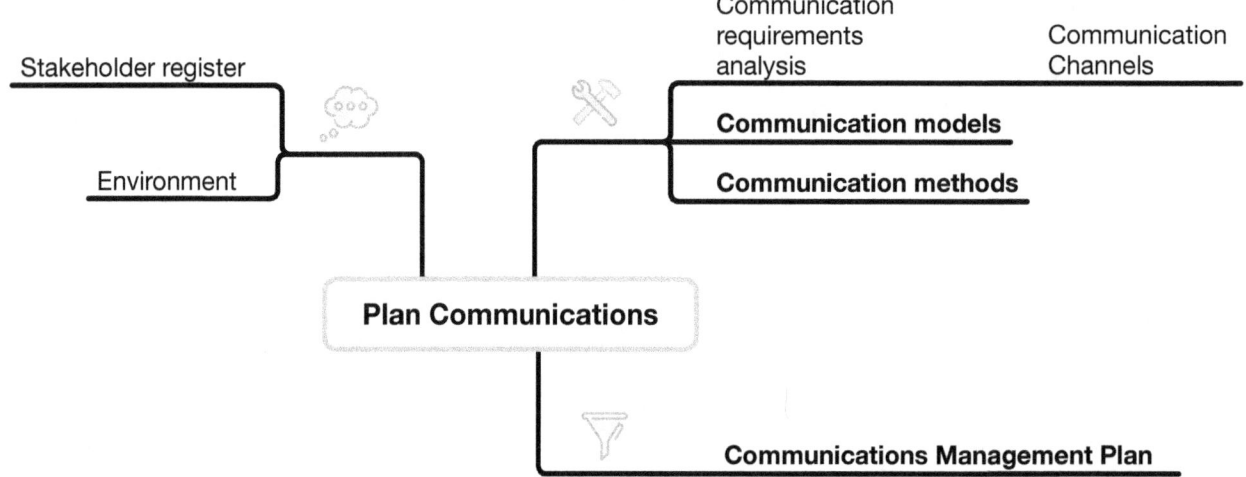

MANAGE COMMUNICATIONS

Knowledge Area	:	Communications Management
Process Group	:	Executing
Focus on	:	Doing meetings as per the plan Sending notes/escalations
Keywords	:	**Timely and appropriate communication.** **Creation, distribution, and disposal of project Information**

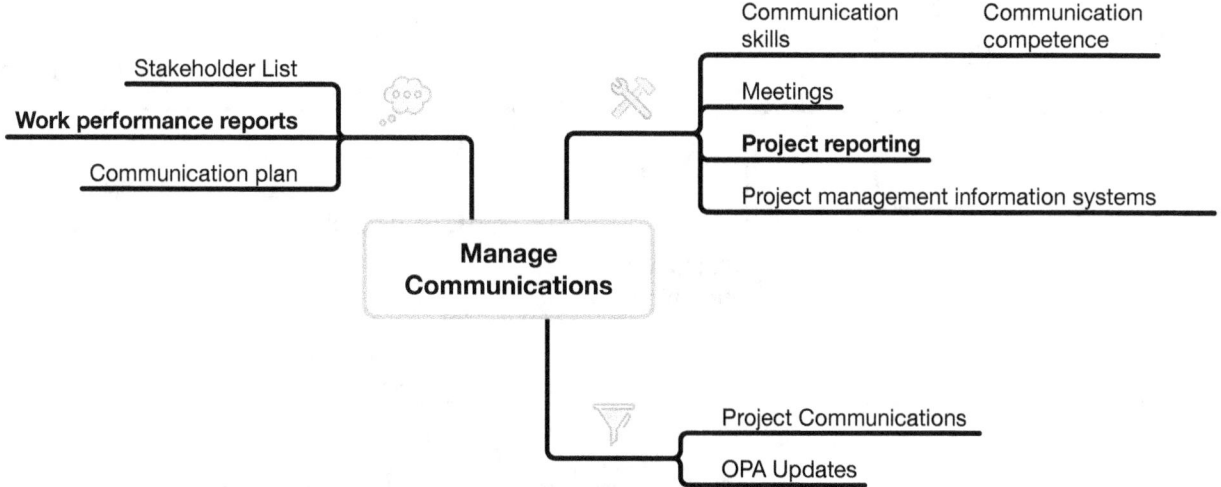

MONITOR COMMUNICATIONS

Knowledge Area	:	Communications Management
Process Group	:	Monitoring and Controlling
Focus on	:	Optimizing Information exchange.
Keywords	:	**Checking stakeholder and information needs**
		Optimizing information exchange

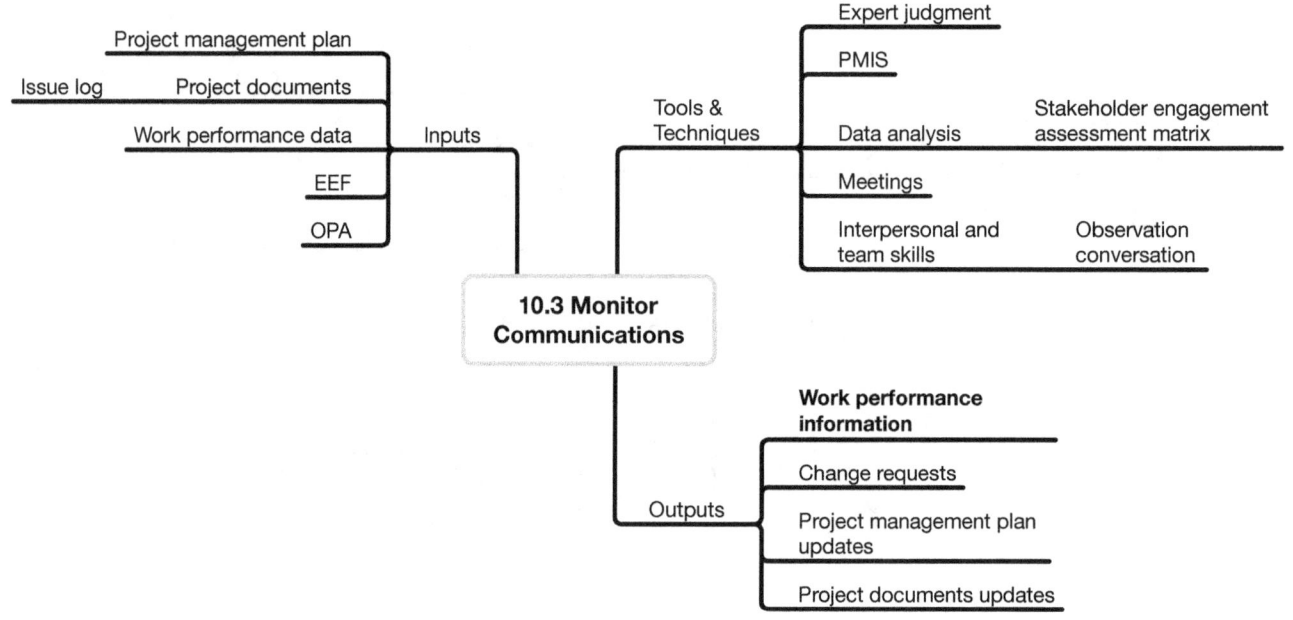

RISK MANAGEMENT

Project Risk Management includes identifying, analyzing, and managing risks on the project. Risk management aims to **reduce threats and leverage opportunities** when they arise.

No	Process Name	Process Group
11.1	Plan Risk Management	Planning
11.2	Identify Risks	Planning
11.3	Perform Qualitative Risk Analysis	Planning
11.4	Perform Quantitative Risk Analysis	Planning
11.5	Plan Risk Responses	Planning
11.6	Implement Risk Responses	Executing
11.7	Monitor Risks	Monitoring & Controlling

PLAN RISK MANAGEMENT

Knowledge Area	:	Risk Management
Process Group	:	Planning
Focus on	:	Defining risk management approach
Keywords	:	**Defining the approach to identify and respond to risk**

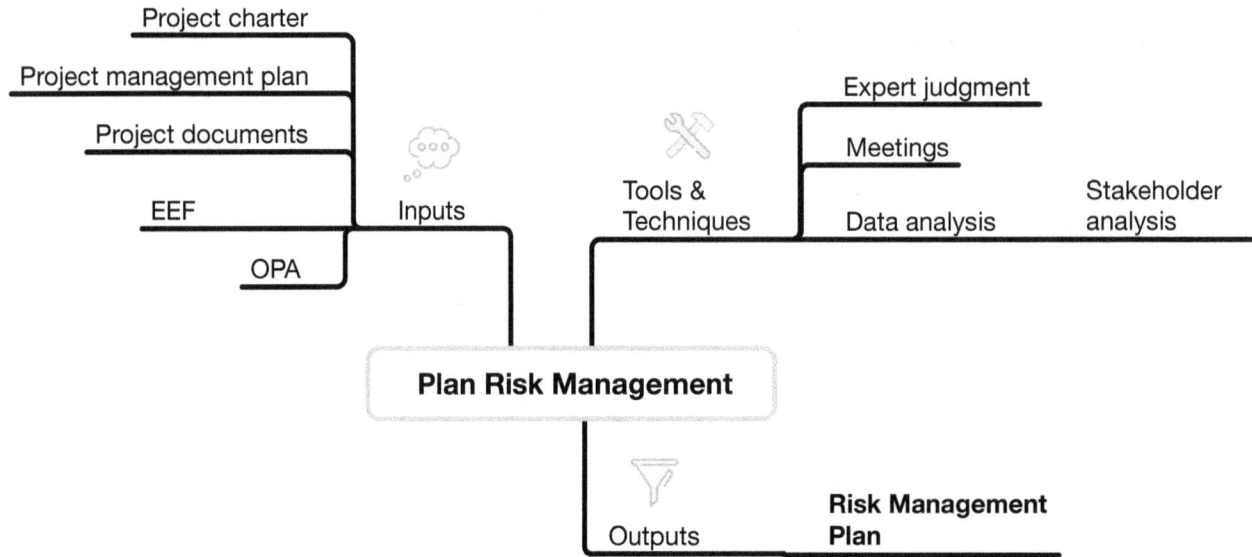

IDENTIFY RISKS

Knowledge Area	:	Risk Management
Process Group	:	Planning
Focus on	:	Identifying risks and Opportunities
Keywords	:	**Identifying individual and overall project risks**
		Documenting the details

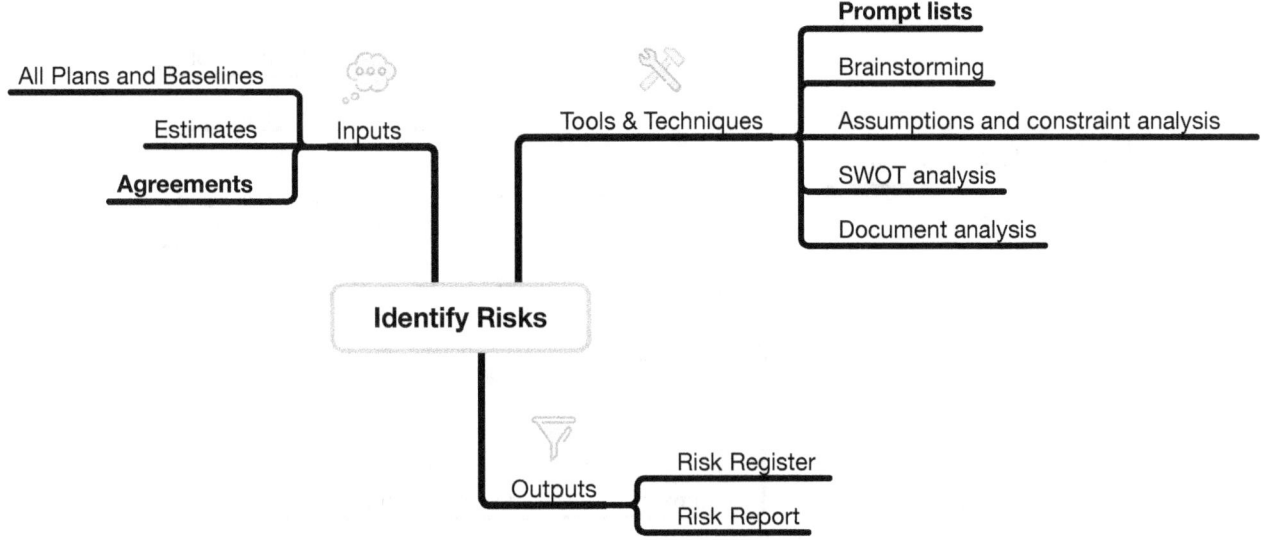

PERFORM QUALITATIVE RISK ANALYSIS

Knowledge Area	:	Risk Management
Process Group	:	Planning
Focus on	:	Prioritize risks
Keywords	:	**Prioritize risks** **Using the probability of occurrence and impact.**

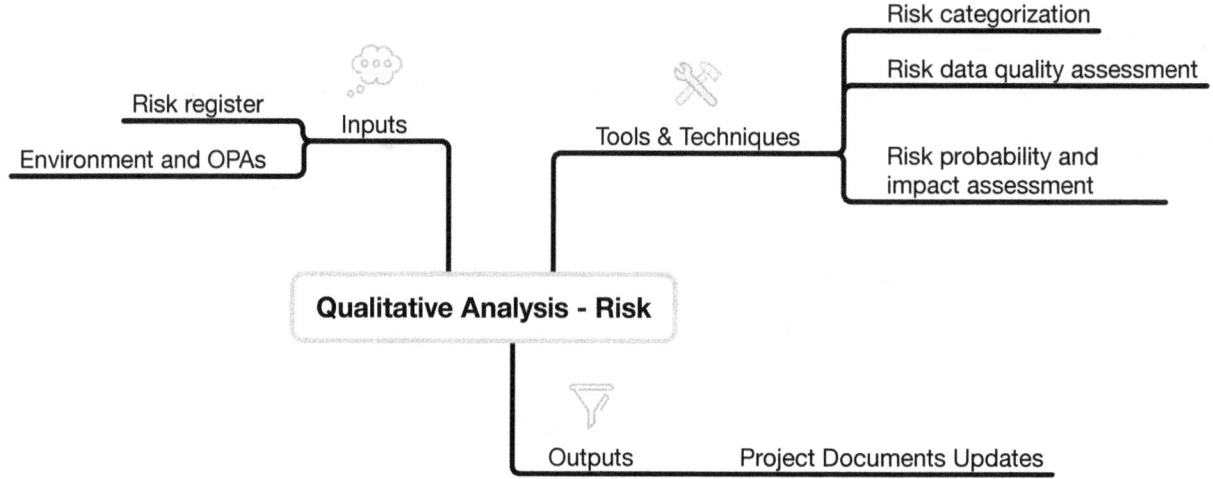

PERFORM QUANTITATIVE RISK ANALYSIS

Knowledge Area	:	Risk Management
Process Group	:	Planning
Focus on	:	Numerically analyzing significant risk, individually.
Keywords	:	**Performed only for very significant risks** **To establish the quantifiable threat.** **Requires a large quantity of data and analysis** **Optional process.**

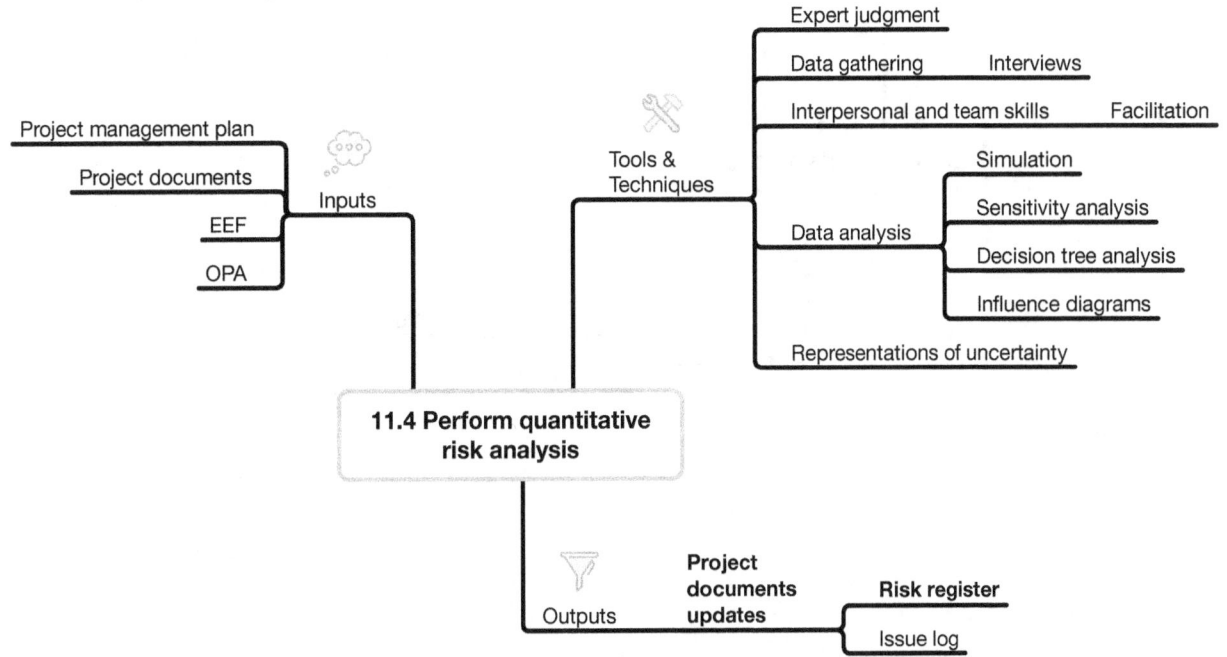

PLAN RISK RESPONSES

Knowledge Area	:	Risk Management
Process Group	:	Planning
Focus on	:	Risk Response planning
Keywords	:	**Enhance opportunities**
		Reduce threats

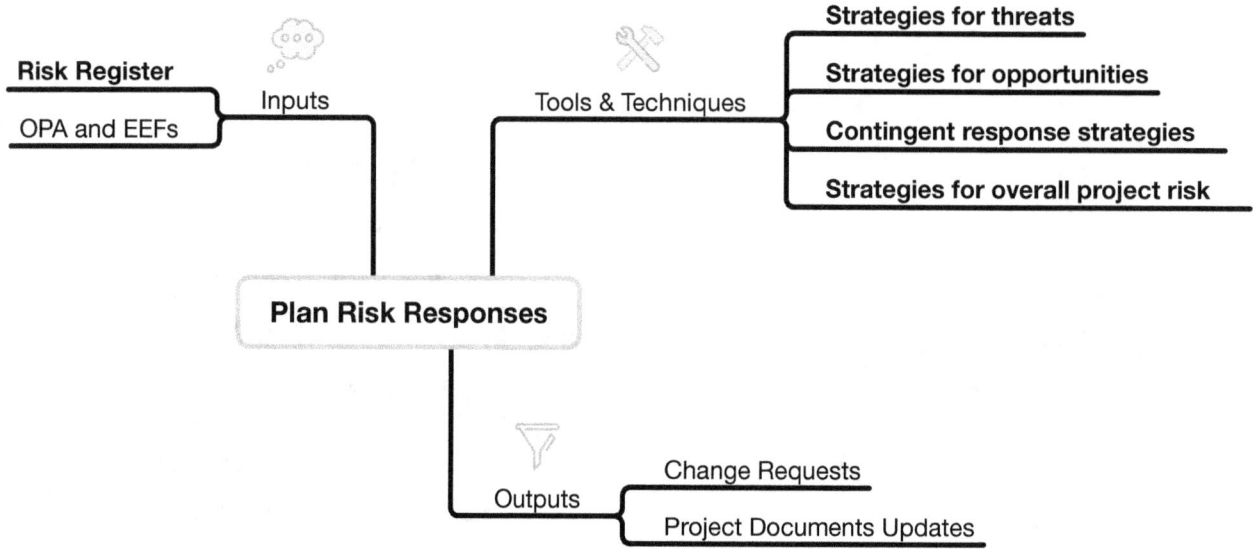

IMPLEMENT RISK RESPONSES

Knowledge Area	:	Risk Management
Process Group	:	Executing
Focus on	:	Implementing planned response for risk events.
Keywords	:	**Implementing agreed-upon risk responses.**

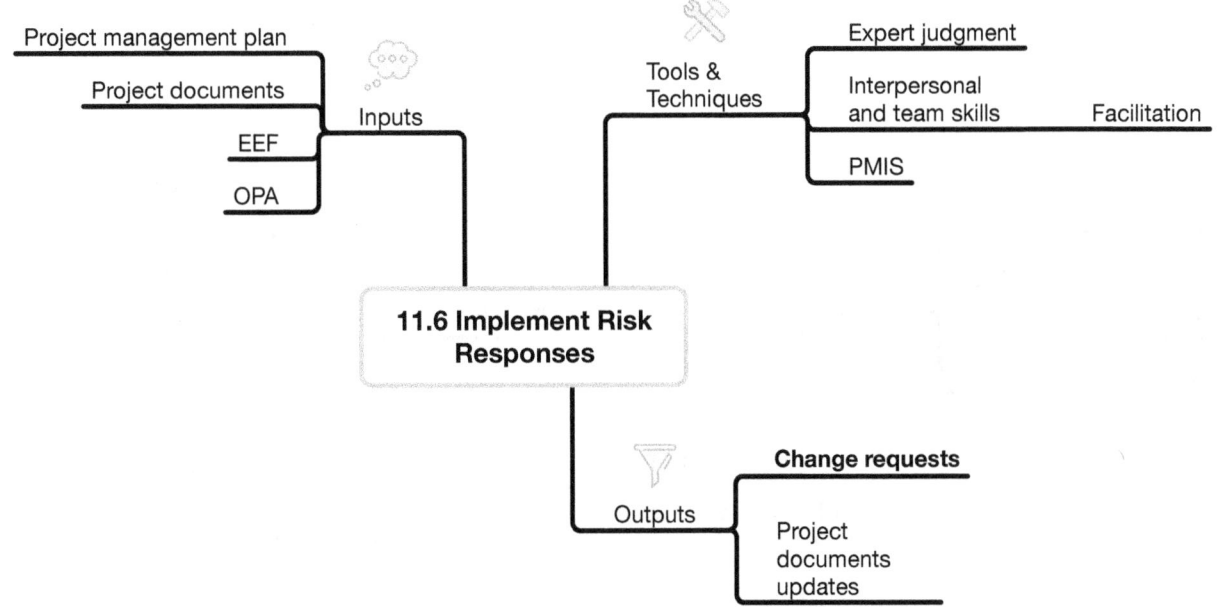

MONITOR RISKS

Knowledge Area	:	Risk Management
Process Group	:	Monitoring and Controlling
Focus on	:	Checking risk management effectiveness
Keywords	:	Monitoring residual risks and identifying new risks. Risk Audits Risk register updates Analyzing old and new risks

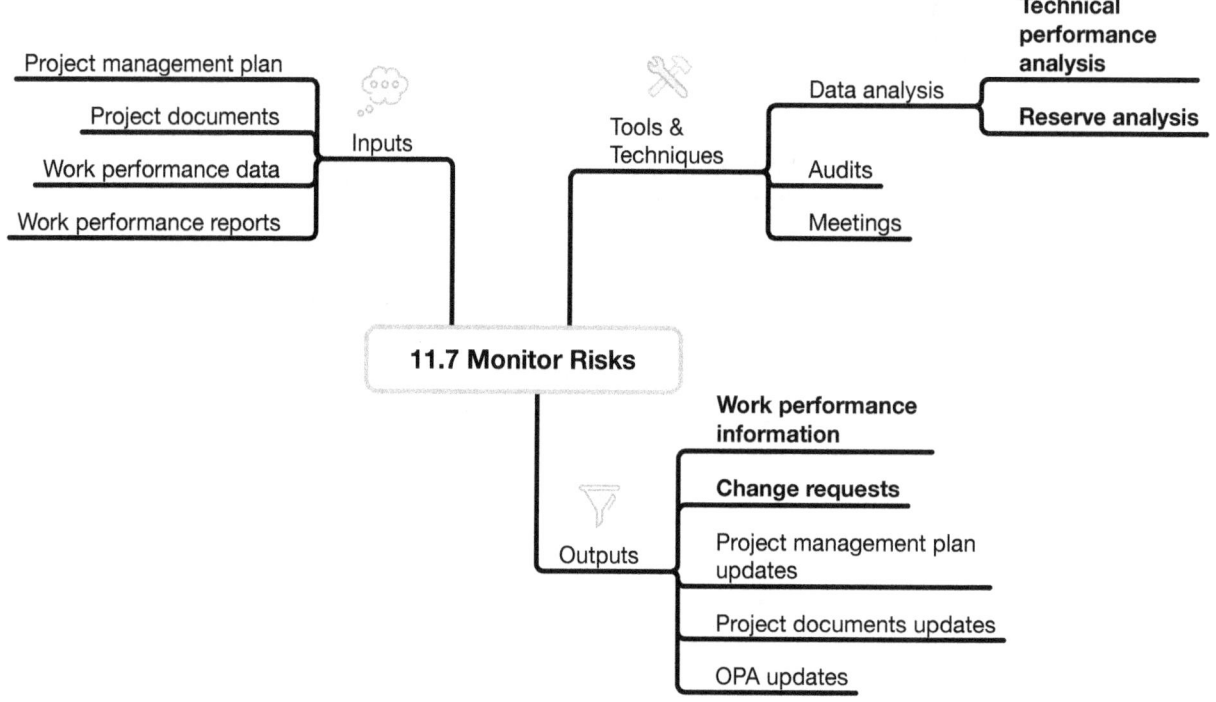

PROCUREMENT MANAGEMENT

Project Procurement Management includes the processes of buying **or acquiring products, services, or results** from outside the project team.

P. No	Process Name	Process Group
12.1	Plan Procurement Management	Planning
12.2	Conduct Procurements	Executing
12.3	Control Procurements	Monitoring & Controlling

PLAN PROCUREMENTS

Knowledge Area	:	Procurement Management
Process Group	:	Planning
Focus on	:	Make or Buy analysis
Keywords	:	**What, how, and when to buy**

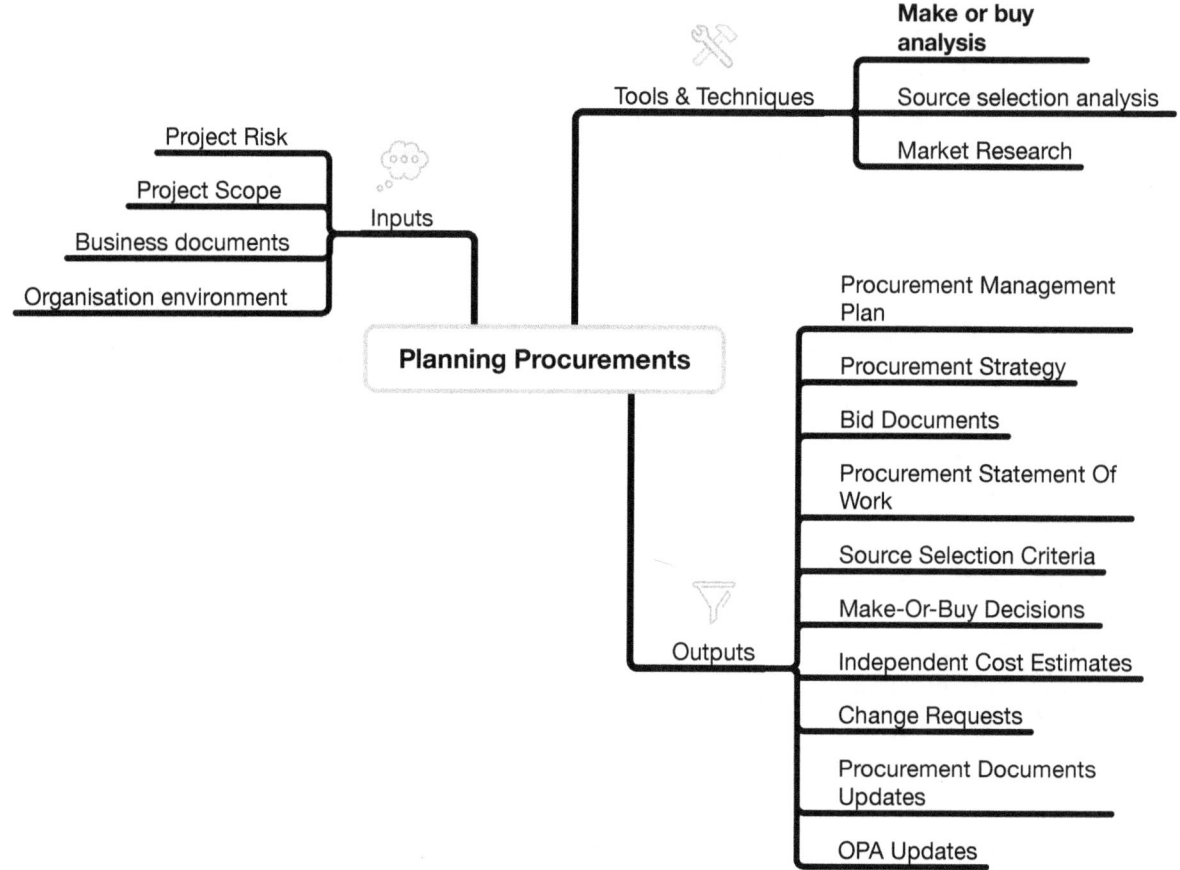

CONDUCT PROCUREMENTS

Knowledge Area	:	Procurement Management
Process Group	:	Executing
Focus on	:	Advertising and Selecting the seller
Keywords	:	**Obtaining seller responses,** **Selecting a seller** **Awarding a contract**

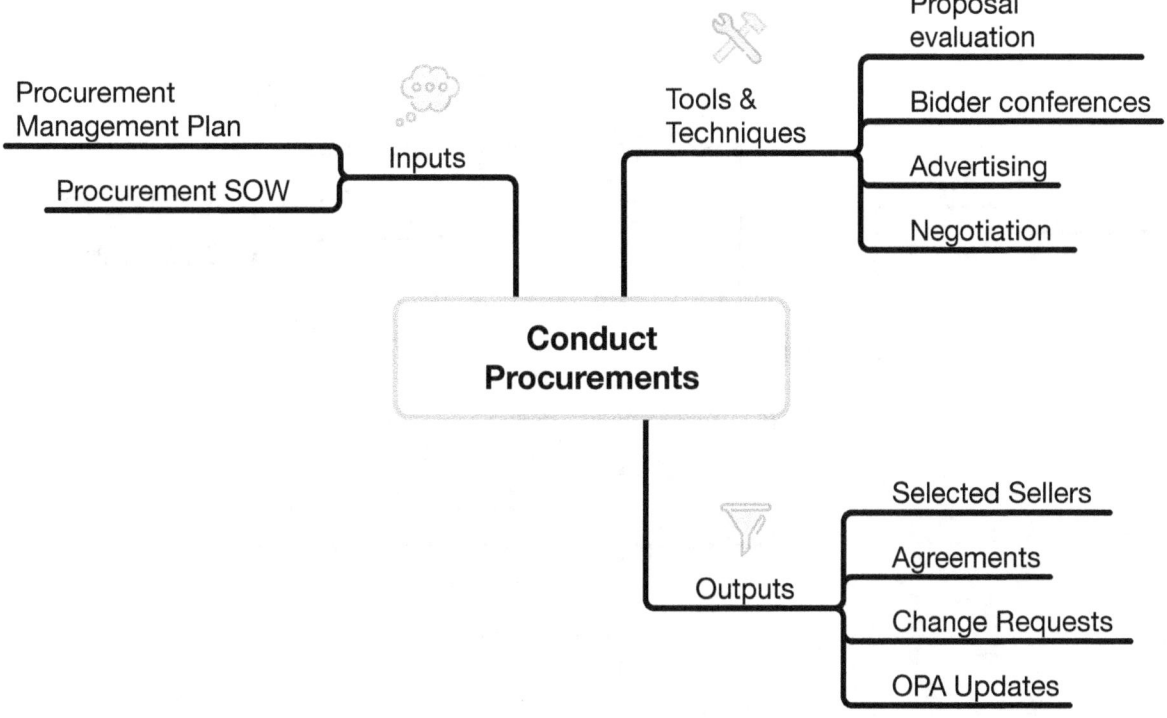

CONTROL PROCUREMENTS

Knowledge Area	:	Procurement Management
Process Group	:	Monitoring and Controlling
Focus on	:	Managing seller performance
Keywords	:	**Managing procurement relationships** **Monitoring contract performance** **Closing the contract.**

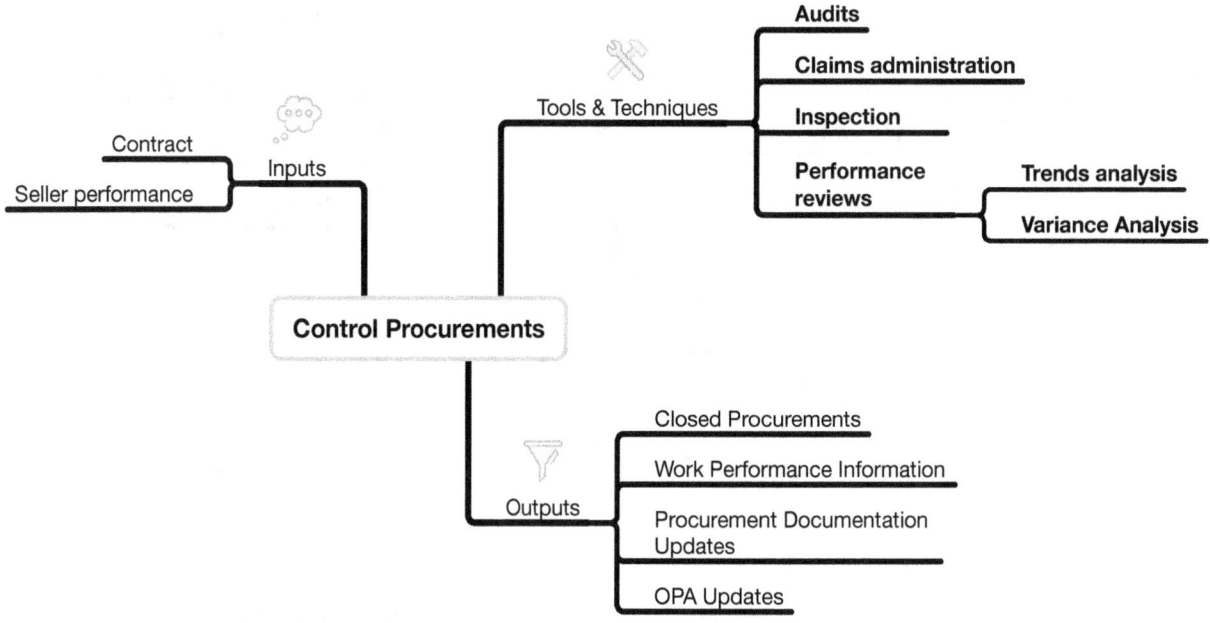

STAKEHOLDER MANAGEMENT

Identifying stakeholders, understanding their expectations, and effectively engaging with them.

P. No	Process Name	Process Group
13.1	Identify Stakeholders	Initiating
13.2	Plan Stakeholder Management	Planning
13.3	Manage Stakeholder Engagement	Executing
13.4	Monitor Stakeholder Engagement	Monitoring & Controlling

IDENTIFY STAKEHOLDERS

Knowledge Area	:	Stakeholder Management
Process Group	:	Initiating
Focus on	:	Identifying Stakeholders
Keywords	:	**Identifying Stakeholders**
		Understanding their interests, influence, and impact on the project

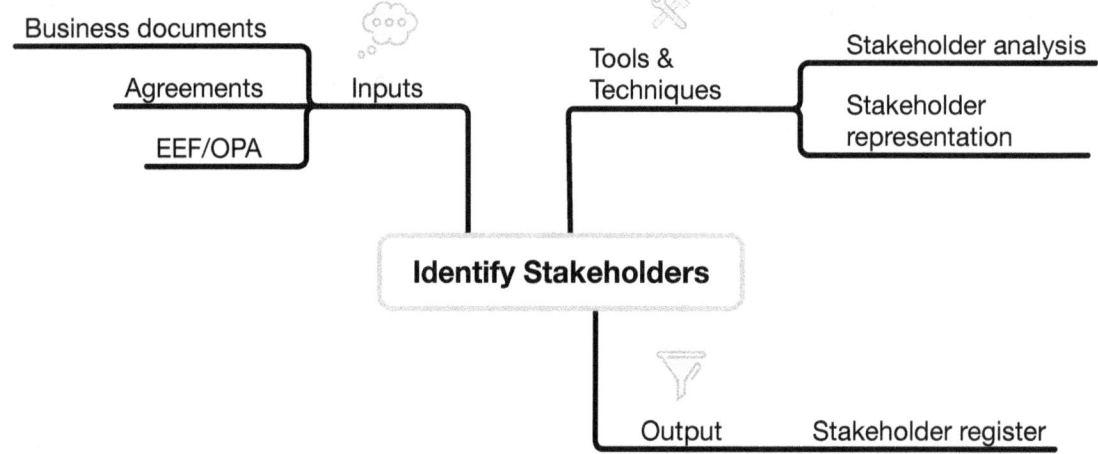

PLAN STAKEHOLDER ENGAGEMENT

Knowledge Area	:	Stakeholder Management
Process Group	:	Planning
Focus on	:	Developing appropriate strategies
Keywords	:	**Developing appropriate management strategies** **Effectively engage stakeholders**

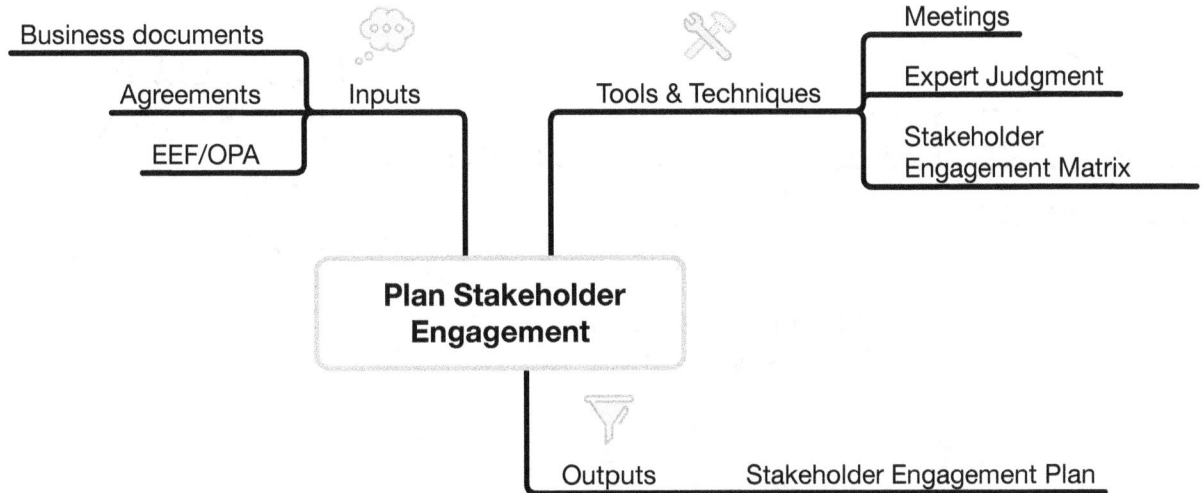

MANAGE STAKEHOLDER ENGAGEMENT

Knowledge Area	:	Stakeholder Management
Process Group	:	Executing
Focus on	:	Meeting/Communicating with Stakeholders
Keywords	:	**Working with stakeholders to address their expectations** **Resolving issues as they occur, and** **Fostering appropriate stakeholder engagement.**

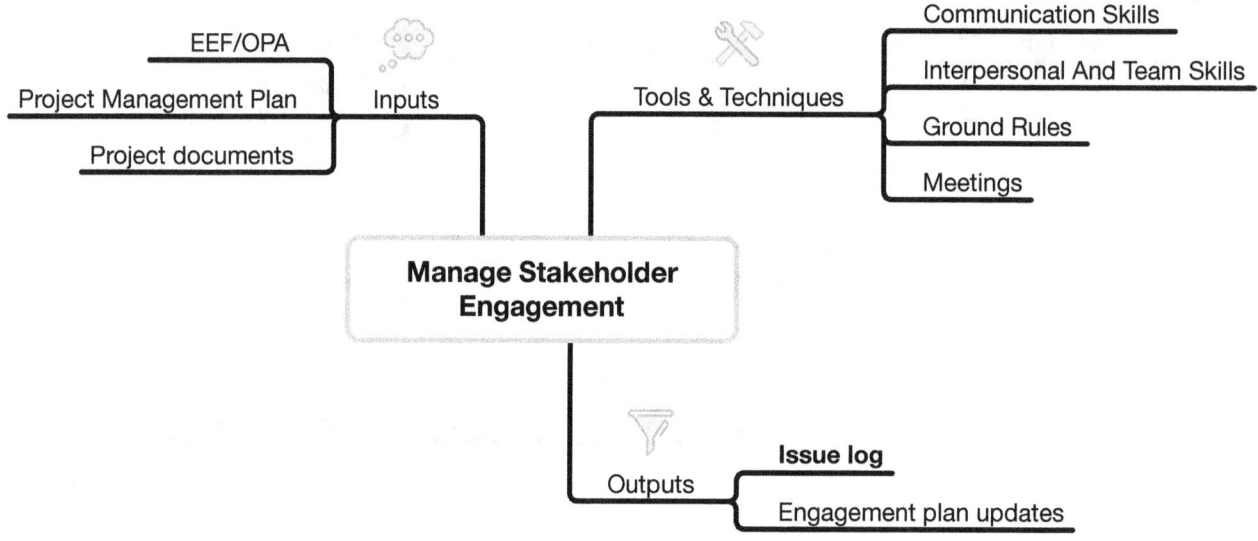

MONITOR STAKEHOLDER ENGAGEMENT

Knowledge Area	:	**Stakeholder Management**
Process Group	:	Monitoring and Controlling
Focus on	:	Adjusting strategies to manage stakeholders
Keywords	:	**Assessing stakeholders' affiliations and adjusting strategies.**

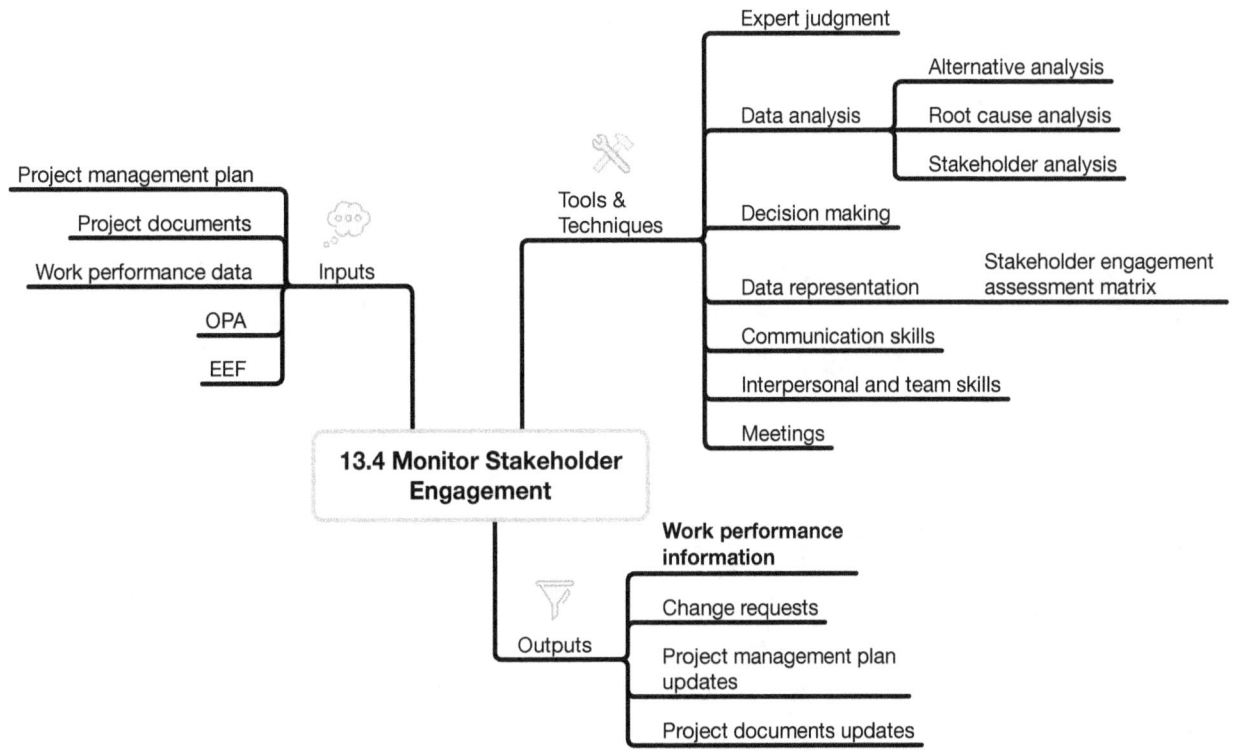

4. Agile Overview and Key Terms

AGILE OVERVIEW

AGILE ARTIFACTS

Product Backlog	The Product Backlog contains required features, errors, or improvements. The Product Owner can compile this list from the competitor analysis, user feedback, and market demands.
Sprint backlog	The sprint backlog is the subset of the Product Backlog. The sprint backlog is the features that have been selected for the current Sprint.
Product increment	The product increment is the outcome prepared by the team in a sprint. It is called increment because it contains the older features produced by the team.

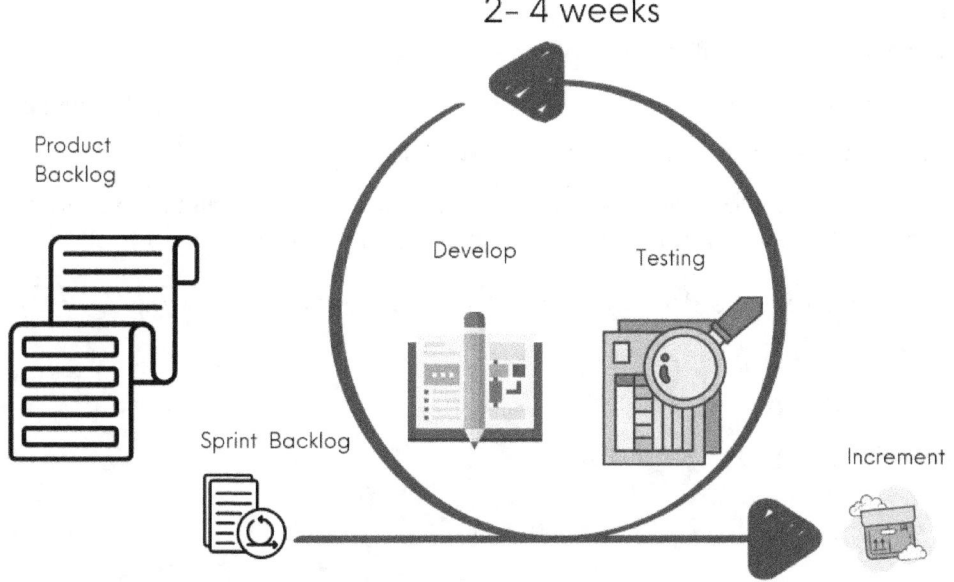

AGILE ROLES

PRODUCT OWNER	The Product Owner owns the product backlog. They own the entire product portfolio and decide on the features, which take more priority than others. A product owner is responsible for grooming the product backlog (prioritizing it) and giving the development team a sense of direction and vision of the product to the development team.
SCRUM MASTER	Scrum Master is the new name for the Project Manager in agile teams. They should show the traits of servant leadership and coordinate with the stakeholders. They are also responsible for ensuring that the development team performs their task by removing impediments, also called issues.
DEVELOPMENT TEAM MEMBERS	T-shaped skillset - enthusiastic individuals who work on building the increments.

AGILE CEREMONIES/EVENTS

SPRINT PLANNING	Time boxed event. This is done at **the start of the iteration** to select the Sprint Backlog Items. The team can use prioritization methods to select the user stories for the Sprint.
DAILY SCRUM	The development team meets daily to **discuss progress** and any **blockers/issues** and update the progress in the burndown chart.
SPRINT REVIEW	The Scrum Team invites stakeholders to discuss and show the sprint deliverables. The Product Owner can release any completed functionality if they feel so.
SPRINT RETROSPECTIVE	During a sprint retrospective, the team discusses the top 3 questions: 1. What went well. 2. What could have been better 3. Any better way of doing things

SCRUM EVENTS

SCRUM Event	Timebox*	Roles to attend	The intent of the Meeting
Sprint Planning Meeting	8 Hours	Product Owner Development Team Scrum Master	Time boxed event. This is done at the start of the iteration to select the Sprint Backlog Items. The team can use prioritization methods to select the user stories for the Sprint.
Daily Stand-ups	15 Mins	Development Team	The Development Team meets daily to discuss progress and any blockers/issues and update the progress in the burndown chart.
Sprint Review Meeting	4 Hours	Product Owner Development Team Scrum Master Other Stakeholders	The Scrum Team invites stakeholders to discuss and show the Sprint deliverables. The Product Owner can release any completed functionality if they feel so.
Sprint Retrospective	3 Hours	Development Team Scrum Master Product Owner (Optional)	During a Sprint retrospective, the team discusses the top 3 questions: 1. What went well 2. What could have been better 3. Any better way of doing things

FEW MORE DEFINITIONS

TIMEBOX	The timebox is an agreed period in which the development team works towards completing the Sprint. The team cannot continue the work beyond the timebox.
BACKLOG GROOMING	The development team works with the product owner to refine the product backlog based on value. Also called **product backlog refinement.**
DEFINITION OF READY	Also called DOR. These would ensure that the product owner and development team do not waste time discussing and selecting the stories for the Sprint. The DOR can follow **INVEST** criteria, i.e., Individual, Negotiable, Valuable, Estimable, Small, Testable for the Product Backlog Items.
DEFINITION OF DONE	Also called DOD. The development team set these criteria to establish the required work for all PBI to be considered complete. E.g., Testing done? Is Peer Review done?
MINIMUM VIABLE PRODUCT	Also called MVP, it is a bare-bone product that can be released in the market to test the product viability and see the acceptance by intended users

5. KEYWORDS - TOOLS AND TECHNIQUES

KEYWORDS - DATA GATHERING TECHNIQUES

Benchmarking	Comparing to a standard
Brainstorming	Ideas
Check Sheets	Data compilation in a standard format
Checklists	Yes/ No in a standard form. An excellent way to implement a standard
Focus Groups	People from Similar domain
Workshops	Cross-domain
Interviews	Pre-Written, One-on-One Discussions
Questionnaires And Surveys	Push communication to gather information from a large population group
Statistical Sampling	Testing on a smaller random population

KEYWORDS - DATA REPRESENTATION TECHNIQUES

Affinity diagrams	**Similar** Ideas
Cause and effect diagrams	**Root-Cause** diagram or Ishikawa diagram
Control charts	Process performance using **UCL and LCL**
Flowcharts	Analyzing the process to optimize it further
Hierarchical charts	Tree-based Graphs, **One to Many relationships**
Histograms	**Comparisons**, Vertical bar chart
Matrix diagrams/Matrix-based charts	Ways to represent data **using T, L, Y, roof, and X shape**
Mind mapping	Using pictures to show **related** ideas
Scatter diagrams	Also called **correlation** diagrams, **Two variables**

KEYWORDS - DATA ANALYSIS TECHNIQUES

Alternative analysis	Finding **alternates**
Cost of quality	Prevention, appraisal, and waste cost, More in quality management
Decision tree analysis	The rationale for opting for a decision
Influence diagrams	How one decision can affect other parameters
Iteration burndown chart	Agile way to show - how much work has been completed so far
Make or buy analysis	Should we buy or develop inhouse
Performance reviews	**Planned vs. actual** performance
Process analysis	analyzing processes, a useful tool is a **flowchart**
Reserve analysis	Checking **contingency reserves** to match the **risks** present in the project
Root-Cause analysis	Understanding **WHY a problem exists**. **Ishikawa** diagrams can be used
Sensitivity analysis	How sensitive is an attribute to risk? Use **Tornado** diagrams
Simulation	Working with the project's **future scenarios** to arrive at a **confidence level** used in case of **uncertainty**
Stakeholder analysis	Analyzing stakeholders on various parameters
Technical performance analysis	Understanding the product performance, the **defects**, etc
Trends analysis	**One variable over a period**, e.g., productivity
Variance analysis	**Planned vs. actual** performance
What if scenario analysis	Checking **various options** and results

6. ABOUT KAVITA SHARMA

Kavita Sharma
Significant Contributor
PMBOK- Sixth Edition

Kavita Sharma has two decades of project management experience in IT, Project Management, Program Management, Account Management, and Project and Leadership Coaching.

She worked with Microsoft, Tech Mahindra, Sapient, and Satyam in her career. While working as an end-to-end program manager, she managed multi-skilled virtual teams ranging from 30 - 90 members having widespread skill sets.

In the last few years (approx. 10), she has evolved as a great mentor to the PMP aspirants and conducts project management workshops. She authored many books, including the best seller:

Pass PMP in 21 Days - Study Guide.

You can see her name in the PMBOK as a significant contributor and CAPM (eLearning by PMI) reviewer.

Her focus is now shifting to mindfulness. We hope to see something new from her pretty soon.

YouTube: https://www.youtube.com/channel/UCLjfEAI-EmgzsDQnXiTth9g

LinkedIn: https://www.linkedin.com/in/kavitasharmapmp

Official Website: https://KavitaSharma.net

THANK YOU

Hi, this is Kavita Sharma. Thanks for buying the book and staying with it till the end. I assume that you have gone through the book and stayed with it. And that is the reason you are reading this page.

A lot of effort has gone into producing this book.

I keep receiving feedback from people like you and ensure that the feedback is acted upon. That's the reason you see book updates.

The credit goes to all of you.

I hope that you found the book helpful. If there is any feedback do write to me. I will look forward to hearing from you.

You can reach me at kavita.sh@gmail.com.

Thanks, and wishing you success.

Kavita Sharma

Author, Coach, and Thinker

DISCLAIMER

With this book, I have put in my best effort to bring you the right tools to pass the PMP examination. However, this should not be interpreted as a promise or guarantee of your success. Any positive or negative outcome ultimately depends on your competency, commitment, and the overall effort put into the PMP exam preparation.

You have the right tools with you. Use them and pass the PMP exam.

www.ingramcontent.com/pod-product-compliance
Lightning Source LLC
Chambersburg PA
CBHW081625100526
44590CB00021B/3598